Mier Men

THE ADVENTURES AND SUFFERINGS OF THE COLORFUL TEXANS ON THE MIER EXPEDITION

*A book for young people
and adult general readers*

Jo Harper and Josephine Harper

EAKIN PRESS Fort Worth, Texas
www.EakinPress.com

All illustrations, except for maps, are by Jason Eckhardt.
Map on page 166 is by Nadira Lorin.

Copyright © 2011
By Jo Harper & Josephine Harper
Published By Eakin Press
An Imprint of Wild Horse Media Group
P.O. Box 331779
Fort Worth, Texas 76163
1-817-344-7036
www.EakinPress.com
ALL RIGHTS RESERVED
1 2 3 4 5 6 7 8 9
ISBN-10: 1-68179-125-0
ISBN-13: 978-1-68179-125-8

*For Jim and Jamie Julian,
true Texans*

Contents

Acknowledgments v
Introduction vii

Chapter 1: *Before the Capture*....................... 1
Chapter 2: *Texans Get Ready to Rescue the Captives* 6
Chapter 3: *The Battle of Salado Creek* 17
Chapter 4: *The Dawson Massacre* 24
Chapter 5: *Disgrace at the Hondo* 30
Chapter 6: *San Antonio Captives*..................... 34
Chapter 7: *The Republic of Texas
  Challenges Mexico* 36
Chapter 8: *At the Camp* 39
Chapter 9: *On the Trail – Bog, Drought, Flood,
  and Stampede* 44
Chapter 10: *Laredo* 48
Chapter 11: *Somervell Finale* 51
Chapter 12: *The Expedition Divides*.................. 55
Chapter 13: *Cuidad Mier at Last* 59
Chapter 14: *The Mexican Forces* 62
Chapter 15: *Before the Battle* 64
Chapter 16: *The Battle at Cuidad Mier* 68
Chapter 17: *Surrender* 75
Chapter 18: *John C. C. and General Ampudia*.......... 80
Chapter 19: *After the Battle* 84
Chapter 20: *Flacco Is Murdered* 88
Chapter 21: *The Captive Mier Men on the Road* 92
Chapter 22: *Texans Start for Mexico City* 98

Chapter 23: *Texans Make a Break* 105
Chapter 24: *Thomas Jefferson Green Uses Suasion* 110
Chapter 25: *After the Battle at Hacienda de Salado*...... 112
Chapter 26: *In the Mountains* 115
Chapter 27: *Recapture*. 123
Chapter 28: *The Black Bean Episode* 127
Chapter 29: *Survivors March On*. 136
Chapter 30: *Ewen Cameron* 139
Chapter 31: *John C. C. Hill* 141
Chapter 32: *Maverick in Perote* 147
Chapter 33: *Green's Group Arrives at Perote* 150
Chapter 34: *The Fire Eaters Arrive
  in Mexico City* 154
Chapter 35: *Asa Hill's Decision*.................... 158
Chapter 36: *The Prisoners at Molina del Rey* 161
Chapter 37: *Jeffrey Hill*........................... 164
Chapter 38: *Letters Home*......................... 167
Chapter 39: *Escapes from Molina del Rey* 169
Chapter 40: *Escape from Perote* 174
Chapter 41: *Captives Are United at Perote* 179
Chapter 42: *Release of the San Antonio
  Prisoners* 184
Chapter 43: *Bigfoot Is Freed*....................... 186
Chapter 44: *The Men Left Behind* 188
Chapter 45: *Doña Inés de Santa Anna Dies* 190
Chapter 46: *Santa Anna Is Persuaded* 191
Chapter 47: *What Happened to John C.C. Hill
  and Bigfoot Wallace?* 195

Time Line.. 206
Endnotes 209
Glossary... 225
Bibliography 227
Index.. 231

Acknowledgments

Any book of this kind is necessarily indebted to the work of others, and in this particular case we are standing on some very broad shoulders, indeed. Joseph Milton Nance, Archie P. McDonald, and Sam W. Haynes are exemplary scholars whose work we greatly admire—and have greatly drawn from. Interested readers are referred to their work for fuller and more scholarly treatment of the Somervell and Mier Expeditions. We have also drawn from journals, diaries, newspapers, and other accounts. In these cases we have tried to preserve the color and phrasing of the original as far as possible, using direct quotations where we could and paraphrasing as closely as we could when a direct quotation would have been too long or unwieldy.

We owe thanks to Therese Griffiths, Molly Anderegg, and De Aaon Miller for their early reading of the manuscript. We wish to give special thanks to Lalo Julian for helping us simplify and clarify the book.

Author's Note

Dr. Josephine M. Harper, a fine scholar and my loyal daughter, contributed so substantially to the organization and writing of this book as to merit both the position of second author and my undying gratitude.

Second Author's Note

It has always been a pleasure and a privilege to tag along behind the senior author, and riding shotgun on this adventure was certainly no exception.

Introduction

This is the true story of a group of Texas adventurers who invaded Mexico, fought a battle, surrendered, walked to Mexico City in chains, and were imprisoned in Perote Castle. Their ordeal, especially having to draw beans in a lottery for their lives, has captured the imaginations of Texans through the years.

Much of their story is not known; sources are fragmentary, and often contradictory. Still, when the fragments are pieced together, a fascinating tale emerges. It is a tale of the pain men will endure in pursuit of glory—a story of bravery and foolhardiness in the service of honor.

Neither Robert M. Bartlett nor Fanny Chambers Gooch-Iglehart are professional historians. Both use such long quotations as to throw their accuracy into question. However, their contributions are not negligible. Bartlett, whose wife was a descendent of John C. C., relies on personal family letters and on family stories. Family photographs and several letters are reproduced in *Those Valiant Texans*. We spoke to one of John C. C.'s aged relatives, but were unable to examine the documents personally.

John C. C. Hill chose Gooch-Iglehart to write his story and spent a full day telling it to her. He wanted it presented to children in a way that was not biased against Mexicans. Gooch-Iglehart's Victorian tone seems false to contemporary ears, but the tone cannot fully discredit the book. It might be viewed not as a historical document but as how John C. C. wished to be remembered.

Other sources were written or told by the participants long after the events occurred. Some of them reflect the desire to spin a good yarn or to paint themselves in a heroic light more than to convey historical accuracy. However, they clearly reflect the writers' values and reveal their personalities.

The people in this story illustrate the contradictions in human nature. They were kind and cruel; gentle and violent; humorous and pitiable; courageous and foolish; idealistic and self-seeking. In the midst of dishonor, they valued honor above all. They laughed at discomfort, cared little for pain, and tossed their lives away like egg shells. They were too remarkable, too colorful to forget. They were the San Antonio captives, the Dawson and Somerville men, and the men who fought at Mier. In this book, we have grouped them together as The Mier Men.

CHAPTER 1

Before the Capture

This is the true story of a small group of Texas adventurers, the Mier men, who invaded Mexico, fought a battle at Cuidad Mier, surrendered, walked to Mexico City in chains, and were imprisoned in Perote Castle. They had volunteered to invade Mexico because the Mexican army had marched to San Antonio and captured Sam Maverick and other Texas government officials. The volunteers wanted to rescue the captives and bring them back. Their ordeal, especially having to draw beans in a lottery for their lives, has captured the imaginations of Texans through the years. The youngest of the volunteers was John Christopher Columbus Hill, thirteen years old. Also among the volunteers was legendary Texas Ranger, Bigfoot Wallace. The time of these events is 1842-1844.

What Was Happening in the Years before the Capture

Mexican independence. On September 16, 1810, Father Miguel Hidalgo y Costilla made his famous battle cry or *grito*. From the steps of a church in the village of Dolores, he shouted, "Long live the Virgin of Guadalupe, death to bad government, death to Spaniards." (Herring 255) This call for rebellion is considered the beginning of the Mexican War of Independence from Spain. Unlike the war of independence

1

2 Mier Men

fought by the North American colonies against England, the Mexican war of independence was not a single, organized war. Rather, it a series of rebellions caused by unrest in both Spain and Mexico. At last, after more than ten years, Spain granted independence to Mexico on August 24, 1821.

At the time of the Mier Expedition, some twenty years later, Mexico was a new and troubled nation. It was weak, and poorly prepared for governing. Most of its time and money were spent in trying to control the revolts that continued to erupt. It is easy to see why the Texan movement for independence was thought of as only another revolt, or as Santa Anna believed, an Anglo-American attempt to seize land for the United States. It is equally easy to see how the Texans felt no loyalty to the new government. It was one of many governments seizing power during these years, and it was harsh in its efforts to keep order.

Texas' independence. President Santa Anna of Mexico had signed papers agreeing to Texas' independence after he was captured in the Battle of San Jacinto in 1836. Texas became a republic. However, Mexico never considered Santa Anna's agreement to be fair and legal. From the Mexican viewpoint, his signature was forced, and Texas was fighting against its true government.

Santa Anna sent troops into Texas under General Vasquez in March 1842 and under General Woll in September of the same year. He wanted to show the Texans that Mexico still considered them rebellious Mexicans, not citizens of an independent country.

Many of the Mexican leaders realized that Mexico could not keep Texas; it was bound to break away. It was too far away from Mexico City to be governed easily, and it had been largely settled by people of a different culture who were used to governing themselves. However, for political reasons, even these leaders found it necessary to support the popular idea that Mexico should fight to keep Texas.

The year was still new when rumors that there would be a Mexican attack reached the Tejanos, the Spanish-speaking Texans, in San Antonio. They warned their Anglo friends that an invasion was likely and that they should run to safety.[1] Sam Maverick acted on his friends' advice and moved his family to a safer place near Buckner's Creek in February 1842. Others followed. By August no more than thirty Anglos remained in San Antonio.[2]

Fear of Mexican attack had also struck the town of Gonzales, about seventy-five miles east of San Antonio. In March, families sent their boys galloping on horseback to bring in the livestock that they let roam and graze freely. The frightened settlers abandoned Gonzales and herded the animals to a settlement on the Colorado River, fifty miles away. Among the fleeing settlers were Baptist preacher Zenos Morrell, his wife, and his son, Allen.

Santa Fe Expedition

Mexico had good reason to believe that Texas was a threat and would take its territory. In 1841, Texas had laid claim to the Mexican territory of New Mexico. President Mirabeau B. Lamar wanted to secure the Texan claim. Without the approval of the Texas Congress, Lamar arranged an expedition to Santa Fe. This would establish a trade route and would offer the New Mexicans the chance to participate in Texas government. He called for volunteers to join the expedition, promising merchants transportation and protection for their goods.

On June 19, 1841, the disastrous Santa Fe expedition left with twenty-one ox-drawn wagons and 321 men. The men suffered from hunger, thirst, and problems with Indians. They got lost along the way. When they finally reached Santa Fe, sick and exhausted, they were amazed to find that they were not welcome. An army met them, and, without a single shot being fired, the expedition passed into Mexican hands. The Texans were marched to Mexico City and imprisoned.

4 Mier Men

The Capture

In early September 1842, Sam Maverick and other officials who had fled San Antonio for fear of a Mexican attack, left their families safely behind at Buckner's Creek and returned to the city. They had legal business that was important enough to make them risk the danger, but they felt increasingly uneasy. At dawn on September 11, they were jarred awake by the sound of cannon shot. The Mexican invasion they had so long feared was upon them.

Heavy fog covered the city. From Maverick's house at one corner of the plaza, Texans fired at the moving shapes. When the fog lifted, the Texans found that they were surrounded by Mexican troops. They were shocked when they discovered the size of the force. A mere sixty Texans faced 1,300 Mexican soldiers. John Twohig, thirty-six-year-old merchant and banker, hastily blew up his store to keep supplies from the enemy.

The Texans were too badly outnumbered to resist further, but they told the Mexican commander, General Woll, that they had thought they were defending themselves against a band of robbers, not resisting a lawful army. They surrendered as *prisoners of war*, a status that was supposed to guar-

---

Maverick

Samuel Augustus Maverick became a Texas land owner, held government offices, and was the father of one of Texas' most influential families. He was born in 1803, the son of Samuel and Elizabeth Maverick. His father had a plantation in Pendleton, South Carolina. Maverick's early education was at home, but he graduated from Yale in 1825 and received a Virginia law license in 1829. He developed a sharp business sense by handling financial affairs for his father. He moved to Texas in 1835. He was one of the few emigrants who was not driven by necessity, thirst for revenge, or hunger for glory. He was interested in building a financial empire and in making Texas part of the United States. He played a part in the Texas Revolution from Mexico, but opposed the South's secession from the United States. He kept a diary that provides a vivid and important record of the time.

antee that they would be well treated. They were also promised a recommendation for their early release.[3]

What was Texas Like?

Land was abundant, cash was scarce, and life was hard. The population of the new Republic of Texas was small and scattered. It contained the towns of Galveston, Houston, Marshall, Austin, and Gonzales along with a number of villages and settlements such as Seguin and La Grange. The major city was San Antonio, which had 2,000 inhabitants, 200 of them Anglos.

Young men came to the new republic looking for fortune and adventure. Most were penniless. All were used to hardship and cared little for comfort.

Settled families kept domestic animals and had gardens, but they did not know how to preserve food by canning. They dried beans and corn and stored potatoes for winter. People on the move carried flour, sugar, and dried meat with them.

Desperados fled from the law in other states and preyed on the settlers. There were so many horse thieves that it was almost impossible to keep mounts, and Indian raids were a regular part of life.

The Texas Rangers

The Republic of Texas needed a police force, so in 1840, President Sam Houston commissioned young Jack Coffee Hays to form the Texas Rangers. Hays was told to recruit 150 men to Ranger service. He found that impossible. Not many men who could afford a horse and gun were willing to work for little more than hardship and danger. He was only able to recruit fifty Rangers. Some Lipan Apaches also joined him as scouts and fighters.[4] The Rangers came to be police force, army, and legend. In the words of one observer, a Texas Ranger could "ride like a Mexican, trail like an Indian, shoot like Tennessean, and fight like the devil."[5]

CHAPTER 2

Texans Get Ready to Rescue the Captives

Ranger Bigfoot Wallace

In San Antonio, late in the summer of 1842, Texas Ranger Bigfoot Wallace, twenty-five, had observed a group of about a dozen Mexican strangers behaving suspiciously. He had heard the rumors about a possible invasion, and wondered if the strangers were connected with the Mexican Army. Then he discovered that there was no ammunition for sale anywhere in San Antonio. Bigfoot and Ranger Nathan Mallon headed to Austin to buy ammunition. Austin was eighty miles away, and there was not a single house on the road there.

When Bigfoot and Mallon arrived, they found that an Indian raid had so terrified the settlers that no one dared to go outside of town. The bodies of two men killed in the raid had been left lying out on the open prairie because the people were too afraid to go out to retrieve them. Bigfoot and Mallon brought the bodies into Austin, buried them, bought what ammunition they could, and then left to return to San Antonio. Bigfoot carried a keg of gunpowder rolled in a blanket and tied to his saddle horn; Mallon carried a supply of caps and lead.

They detoured to a ranch just outside Seguin to get corn for their horses. They were surprised to find Rangers Rice and Johnson at the ranch, sitting on the ground, with two Tejana women picking cactus thorns out of their bare feet.

Bigfoot laughed at the sight, but Rice and Johnson had grim news. They had thorns in their feet because a group of Mexican cavalry had chased them through the cactus. They told Bigfoot and Mallon that San Antonio was in Mexican hands and that sixty Texans had been taken captive. Rice and Johnson had fought with Mexican soldiers outside San Antonio and had killed the Mexican bandmaster and General Woll's horse.

Volunteers were gathering at Seguin to pursue the Mexican army and rescue the captives. Bigfoot hurried to join the volunteers.

The Hills Join the Volunteers

A lone rider galloped to the Hill family's farm outside Fayetteville later that September. He brought the bitter news

---

Bigfoot

John Duval and A. J. Sowell both wrote biographies of Bigfoot Wallace, and both knew him personally. Duval actually served with him in the Rangers. A. J. Sowell was a generation younger, but his father had served with Wallace. Both biographies are based on personal interviews, but the biographers tell different stories of how Bigfoot got his name. Duval said it was because when Wallace was in Mexico, his feet seemed big to the Mexicans. According to Sowell, Wallace denied this and said that there were other men on the long march who had bigger feet than he did. There was also a rumor that Wallace acquired the name "Bigfoot" because he killed an Indian by that name. He denied this as well.

Wallace told Sowell that in 1839 when he lived in Austin, the area was plagued by an Indian called "Bigfoot." His tracks measured "fourteen inches with his moccasins on" and "were also distinctive because the big toe in his right moccasin was always out and showed its imprint in the soil." (Sowell, 1989, 29-33)

One night the Indian came to town and went into the house of a man named Gravis. Then he went to Wallace's house. The next morning, Gravis tracked the footprints to Wallace's door and accused him of breaking into his kitchen. Wallace also wore moccasins, but when he put his foot in the track, his foot was smaller and the toe wasn't out. Gravis apologized and also gave Wallace the name by which he became famous.

of the Mexican invasion and capture of Sam Maverick and other officials. He told them that volunteers were gathering to free the captives. The Hills had to help.

That evening, Abraham Webb Hill, affectionately known as Asa, sat at the supper table and considered the problem. As head of a large family of sons, he had to decide who should aid in the rescue. It was harvest time and everyone was needed on the farm, but Asa decided that they could spare two men. Who should go?

It could not be Joseph Mendes, the adopted boy who was the Hill's thirteenth child. Joseph had played the fife in the Mexican army, and James Monroe Hill had captured him during the famous Battle of San Jacinto that gave Texas her independence. Joseph Mendes had begged not to be sent back to Mexico, so James Monroe Hill took him home, and the Hills adopted him.

Perhaps thirteen-year-old John Christopher Columbus Hill looked at his friend Joseph Mendes and wondered how it felt to have a foot on both sides of the border. Asa would never ask Joseph Mendes to fight against his own people, but someday Joseph might face that decision. What would he do then? How would he feel?

John C. C. could never have expected to face such a problem himself. His own loyalties were simple and clear. He was pure Texan and proud of it.

Asa was fifty-five years old and had already served in the Texas Revolutionary Army, but he announced that he would go. Jeffrey Barksdale Hill, twenty-eight, would go also because he was the only adult son who had not yet fought for Texas.

John Christopher Columbus Hill spoke up. "I'm going, too!"[1]

John C. C.'s mother objected, but he drew himself up and spoke firmly. "I can ride as well as any man in Texas, and I can outshoot most of them. Besides, I have to look after Papa and Jeff."

In response, John C. C.'s brother, James Monroe Hill, rose

from the table, walked across the room, and took his rifle off the wall. It was the gun he had used in the Battle of San Jacinto six years earlier. He carried the treasured rifle lightly in both hands, stretched out his arms, and presented the gun to John C. C.

"Now it is yours. Never let it fall into Mexican hands."

It was a solemn moment.

John C. C. took the rifle. "Santa Anna's soldiers will never shoot this gun," he vowed, "and I promise to take care of Papa and Jeff."

To the Hills it seemed like the will of God that John C. C., only thirteen years old and small for his age, should go help rescue the captive Texans.

John C. C. would join the volunteers, and he would never forget his vow.

10 Mier Men

Woods Fort

The Woods Join the Volunteers

Old Zadock Woods galloped full speed around Woods' Fort, his rifle raised high above his head. News of the San Antonio capture had reached Woods' Fort, and old Zadock was determined to ride to the captives' rescue. Kind and sensible Norman Woods had done everything in his power to persuade his sixty-nine-year-old father to stay home, but this wild ride was part of Zadock's defiant reply. When he rounded the fort, he leaped off his horse and gave the rest of his answer in words. "I fought with General Jackson at New Orleans and with General Houston at San Jacinto, and I must give them one more crack at Old Zadock."[2]

So despite his misgivings, Norman, thirty-six, went along with his father. So did his brother, Gonzalvo, twenty-seven, and his nephew, Milvern Harrell, eighteen. They joined Mosby Dawson's volunteers under the Muster Oak in La Grange.[3]

Zenos Morrell Joins the Volunteers

In September of 1842, the people of Gonzales were still camping in their temporary settlement on the Colorado River. They needed to harvest their crops if they were to survive the winter, but they still feared a Mexican invasion.

Baptist preacher Zenos Morrell and his son Allen took a wagon and went back to Gonzales to gather their corn. It was dangerous to go there, but they had to have the corn to survive. Zenos and Allen spent several days harvesting. Then, with their wagon loaded, they started back to the settlement. On the road, they met Colonel Mathew Caldwell,[4] known as Old Paint because of the grey spots in his dark red beard. He was forty-three years old, a signer of the Texas Declaration of Independence, and a distinguished soldier.

Caldwell showed Morrell a letter: "Colonel:—General Woll has arrived at San Antonio with thirteen hundred men. The court, judge, jury, lawyers,—and many citizens in attendance are prisoners in the hands of the Mexicans. I made my escape and came round under the mountains to Seguin. John W. Smith."[5]

"Something must be done quick, and you must go with me," Colonel Caldwell told Brother Morrell.[6]

Morrell didn't want to go with him. He had good reasons, and he gave them. He was in poor health. He didn't have a horse. He was badly needed at home.

Old Paint Caldwell, who had been released from the prison at Mexico's Perote Castle just four months earlier, appealed to Morrell's patriotism. Texas needed him.

For Morrell, that was a powerful appeal. Originally from Tennessee, he had been a friend of Tennessean Davy Crockett, the slain hero of the Alamo. He was also a friend of Tennessean Sam Houston, President of the Republic of Texas. Morrell was as ardent in his love of Texas as they, and had vowed to "rise and fall with Texas."[7]

Morrell remembered his vow. He sent his teenage son, Allen, back to the settlement with the corn. It was a dangerous mission for the boy. He had to go fifty miles alone through Indian country in a slow wagon. Morrell went to Seguin with Colonel Caldwell. He had no idea that his own infectious patriotism would prove even more dangerous to young Allen than the hazards of the trail.

In Seguin

Seguin, about thirty-seven miles from San Antonio, was humming with excitement. Men cleaned rifles, molded bullets, and bargained for horses. Almost all of the horses in town had been stolen in an Indian raid, so even the most ordinary ponies brought high prices and were the source of conflict. Two men fought so fiercely over a stray horse that neither of them could use it — the fight had left each of them unable to ride.[8]

Amidst the hubbub, some men tried to take the keg of powder Bigfoot had fetched from Austin. He said he would shoot the first man that laid hands on it. Soon Major Jack

Hays and his lieutenant, Henry McCulloch, arrived and divided the powder and ammunition among the men. The group was made up of Rangers, volunteers, and Indian allies.

Zenos Morrell was able to borrow a horse and join the volunteers. His horse was a fine animal, but untrained. He prepared for the journey to San Antonio by mixing ten ears of parched, ground corn with two pounds of sugar. This mixture was called *cold flour* and could be eaten dry or stirred into a little water.

On the Move to San Antonio and to Salado Creek

Jack Hays and his Rangers led the way to San Antonio. Old Paint Caldwell followed with the 200 volunteers he had gathered together in Seguin. Twenty miles outside the city, the volunteers stopped and selected thirteen of their number to go closer to the town and join Hays. Zenos Morrell was one of the thirteen selected. Colonel Caldwell and the rest of the men went on to make camp at a spot on Salado Creek.

Indians Join the Volunteers

Flacco. The most significant Indian to join the group was

Jack Hays

John Coffee (Jack) Hays, only twenty-five years old, was slender and quiet. He had good manners, and his boyish face made him look even younger than his years, but his "cold eyes and steady self-confidence bespoke authority." (Hardin 11) His "full forehead was crowned with jet black hair" and "his black eyes flashed decision of character." (Morrell 168) Hays had trained under Deaf Smith, the legendary hero of San Jacinto. He was both skilled and fearless. His good judgment and his ability to inspire loyalty made him an impressive leader. Before his career as a Ranger, Captain Hays had been a surveyor. Zenos Morrell (176) tells that six men with Hays as their leader were out surveying and were attacked by Indians. Hays was so determined to accomplish his surveying task that he kept working – compass in one hand, gun in the other – firing whenever the Indians drew near – until the job was finished.

Flacco, a Lipan Apache scout. He and Jack Hays were close friends. Both were young, brave, handsome, and natural leaders.[9] Flacco wanted to be like Hays, and Hays learned many of the finer points of trailing from Flacco. It was also from Flacco that Hays learned important differences in fighting techniques, such as that Comanches were open-field fighters, but Apaches attacked from ambush. Flacco is quoted by various sources as saying that he and another friend were not afraid to go to hell together, but that Jack Hays was not afraid to go to hell by himself.[10]

Writings of the time describe Flacco as tall and erect, strong and agile. His forehead was well developed, and he wore a circlet of eagle feathers set back so that it revealed his fiercely alert black eyes. He wore a fine string of beads and

---

Bigfoot and the Lipans

Once when Bigfoot Wallace was out hunting near Buckner's Creek, he sat down under a tree to rest. Suddenly a Lipan Indian stepped in front of him. Bigfoot sprang to his feet and drew his gun. He was instantly surrounded by a large group of warriors pointing arrows at him. They signaled for him to put his gun down. Bigfoot refused. He thought he was done for, and he was determined to die fighting.

The Lipan who had startled him was the chief. He signaled the others to go ahead, and he led Bigfoot through thickets and tangled forest to camp. After a council meeting and several speeches, which Bigfoot believed were about whether to kill him or not, an Indian woman took him by the hand, led him to a wigwam, and gave him meat to cook for himself.

He lived comfortably with the Lipan band for two weeks. When he was allowed to go hunting with the chief's son, Bigfoot escaped and headed for the Anglo settlement. People there had thought he must be dead and were looking for buzzard signs.

When the chief learned of the escape, he took a shortcut to the settlement and arrived ahead of Bigfoot. He wanted to see President Sam Houston and make a treaty. Bigfoot agreed to take him to Houston, but the chief was afraid someone would shoot him, so he put part of his blanket around Bigfoot, and they walked together with the blanket around them both. Sam Houston made a treaty with the chief, who declared that Houston was the smartest man he ever saw and that he himself was the second smartest.

(Wallace in Sowell *Life of "Big Foot" Wallace* 20)

numerous silver arm and wrist bands. A waist belt held his hunting knife. His white, knee-length leggings were of buckskin. They had wide fringes and were decorated with red and black painted figures. His moccasins were also decorated with fringe and beads.[11]

In appreciation of his ability and loyalty, the Government of Texas had given Flacco the title of "Colonel and had presented him with a full colonel's uniform, including a sword and a plumed hat. He kept them stored in a rawhide box and wore them on ceremonial occasions.[12]

Other Volunteers Head for Salado Creek

As the men who had gathered in Seguin moved toward San Antonio and Salado Creek, other men from across the Republic of Texas also answered the call to rescue the captives. In Fayette County, Nicholas Mosby Dawson, thirty-four-year-old hero of the battle of San Jacinto, was gathering volunteers. Apparently Dawson learned about General Adrián Woll's capture of the Texans from young Allen Morrell, Zenos Morrell's son. Without his father's knowing it, Allen made the fateful decision to join the volunteers.

The volunteers gathered under the "muster oak" on the square in La Grange. Starting with only fifteen men, their number grew to fifty-one as they rode toward San Antonio.

When John C. C. Hill, his father Asa, and his brother, Jeffrey, got to La Grange, they found that the Dawson men were about fourteen hours ahead of them, and that Colonel Caldwell's volunteers had started even earlier. John C. C. was afraid the fight might be over before they got there. As the Dawson group pushed toward San Antonio, they were joined by Samuel Maverick's slave, Joe Griffin. He came "armed to the teeth, riding a good mule,"[13] and with his pockets full of money. He was headed for Mexico to try to free Maverick. Since there was no slavery in Mexico,[14] he planned to pass himself off as a runaway. He hoped this would keep people from suspecting his true motive for being there. Mrs.

Maverick had offered Griffin his freedom for such loyal service, but he turned the offer down. He said that Maverick had always treated him more like a brother than a slave, and he wanted to continue with him. Griffin was determined to free Maverick no matter what the danger.[15]

Joe Griffin was a highly intelligent and competent man. He had acted as manager of one of Maverick's most demanding farms. Perhaps he felt that he had more security and status in his position with Maverick, even though a slave, than he would have had as a free black in Texas at that time. We can only guess at his reasons; we can never be sure what they were.

Joe Griffin

Joe Griffin had also showed his courage earlier. His personal relationship with the Maverick family appears to have been one of long standing.

Griffin had been owned by Mary Maverick's mother, but went with Samuel and Mary Maverick when they left Alabama for Texas in 1837. On the road to San Antonio, seventeen Tonkawa Indians came into the Maverick camp. They had been fighting the Comanches and were painted and well armed. They proudly showed two scalps, one hand, and several pieces of rotten flesh from various parts of the human body. Griffin stood in front of Mary Maverick's tent with a gun and an ax and yelled, "Come this way if you dare, you devils, and I'll make hash out of you!" (Green in Marks 78)

CHAPTER 3

The Battle of Salado Creek

The Taunting Expedition

Hays and the scouting volunteers joined Caldwell at Salado Creek and made their plans. They did not want to fight at San Antonio where the Mexicans had plenty of supplies and were protected by being in town. They decided to try to draw a few Mexicans away from the larger group of soldiers by shouting insults at them, in the hope that a smaller force would chase them to the Salado Creek. There the high embankment and thicket would gave the Texans an advantage.

Of the 202 horses at the volunteer camp, only thirty-eight were fit for the six mile expedition to San Antonio. This was not only because Indian raids and theft from desperados had made good horses scarce, but because some of the overly eager Texans had ridden their horses too hard. The thirty-eight with adequate horses were Texas Ranger Captain Jack Hays along with twenty four other Rangers including Bigfoot Wallace. Zenos Morrell and twelve other volunteers made up the rest of the group.

Inside the city, General Woll assembled his soldiers to respond. Tejanos in San Antonio were as loyal to the Texas cause as the Anglos were. When General Woll declared that he would kill the Texans on Salado Creek, a Tejana woman told him she knew the Texans, and he better watch out.

18 Mier Men

The Texan volunteers gathered quietly outside San Antonio. When Hays gave the signal, the air filled with shouted insults and with the Texan rebel yell. They expected no more than forty or fifty mounted Mexican soldiers would chase them. Instead, ten times that many appeared. The Texans galloped pell mell toward the volunteer camp with the Mexicans close behind. Even the best of the Texans' horses were tired from riding for a week, but the Mexicans had fine, rested horses they had taken from the people of San Antonio. The Texans were able to put themselves about half a mile ahead by cutting through timber land, while the large company of Mexicans stayed on the open prairie. The Texans scattered hats, blankets, and overcoats behind them in their mad race toward the Salado. When Hays and his men galloped into camp, not a man was injured or missing, and Caldwell's volunteers lay in wait in a dense thicket in the creek bottom.

Prepare to Fight

For the volunteers at the camp, however, the taunters' arrival was not exactly welcome. The men were hungry, and one of them, French Smith, had found a fat cow, run her into camp, and killed her. While they were broiling beef and looking forward to a real meal, they heard the sound of muskets. They had to leave their food and get ready to fight on empty stomachs. That didn't suit Sol Simmons who was a big fellow and a powerful eater. He had a dozen big pieces of beef cooking on the fire, and he bolted them down without chewing.

Some of the volunteers went out and paraded in a leisurely manner over some knolls that were in the Mexicans' plain sight. They thought this would fool the Mexicans into thinking there were more volunteers than there really were.

Before the battle began, Old Paint Caldwell addressed the men. Tall, slender, with many patches of white in his dark red beard, he made a striking figure. He stood with his shirt sleeves rolled up and swung his rifle in his right hand, "gestuleting conciderable."[1] He told the men that he would never surrender, that he had just returned from the Santa Fe expedition, and that if he were caught fighting against Mexico a second time, he would be killed. He urged the men to make up their minds to fight it out and not raise the white flag of surrender.

His short speech concluded, "Keep cool and recollect what we are fighting for—it is for liberty and our insulted country." Zenos Morrell added, "Shoot low, and my impression before God is that we shall win the fight."[2]

The First Front at Salado Creek

The Mexicans attacked the Texans; the Texans returned fire. Caldwell had formed his men into two ranks under the banks of the river. As one group advanced and fired, the other group loaded their rifles. Old Parson Carroll, a Methodist preacher, stepped up on the bank, fired, and shouted, "God take your souls!" In each assault, the Mexicans broke file and fell back before they got to the thicket.

The Texans joked and sang. They wanted nothing better than to have the Mexicans come toward them and be shot. The whole thing seemed like child's play. They later bragged that the battle was so easy-going, that while the cannon balls passed above them, they went down into a ravine and finished their meal before the Mexicans got back into formation to advance again.[3]

Sol Simmons was the first Texan hit — shot in the stomach. He roared that he was a dead man, and began to throw up beef. The doctor later said it was the most fortunate shot he ever saw. "If it hadn't been for the beef, the bullet would have killed him, and if it had not been for the bullet, the beef would have killed him."[4] Sol recovered, and the bullet, lost in the beef, was never found.

The Second Front at Salado Creek

Some Tejanos were loyal to Mexico. One of these was Vicente Cordova, aged forty-four, of Nacogdoches. He was a wealthy, educated, public official. Cordova led some eighty-five Cherokee Indians against the Texans. The Cherokees crawled into the creek hollow near the volunteers, but the Texans saw them.

Steve Jouett and Simon Cockrell decided to go down the creek, make a few shots on their own, and pick off some of the Indians. The Indians proved to be fierce fighters, and the light-hearted adventure turned heavy. Cockrell escaped and concealed himself in the creek beneath a leaning tree. He stayed under water with only his nose and mouth out. The Indians passed by without seeing him, and Cockrell came back to camp after dark, wet, wounded, and muddy, but alive. His friend, Jouett, was not so lucky. He lay behind, dead.

When the intense fighting began, Ewen Cameron's company held the Indians back. Vicente Cordova was killed, as were many of his band, even though a group of Carrizo Indians came to join him and the Cherokees. Cordova's forces charged the volunteers repeatedly, but they could not drive them from their position.

Fighting was fierce. The severely outnumbered Texans were besieged by Indians, infantry, and cavalry, but they held firm. One daring Mexican charged Bigfoot Wallace, fired in his face, and shouted, "Take that, you cow thief!"[5]

The large ball from the *escopeta* grazed Bigfoot's nose and almost blinded him with smoke. He fired back anyhow, but missed.

Courageous little Henry Whaling, always "active and full of hell" called out, "Damn such shooting!"[6] and fired. His shot hit the soldier Bigfoot had missed.

All the Texans were fighting hard. Old Paint Caldwell, in

Escopetas

The Mexican soldiers were forced into service and were untrained. Moreover, their *escopetas* were Inaccurate. Bigfoot said of them: "*Escopetas* are a short bell-mouth, bull-doggish looking musket, carrying a very heavy ball, which is death by the law when it hits, but that is seldom, for they shoot with little accuracy. They are good for nothing, except to make a noise, and a volley from them always put me in mind of the old saying about shearing hogs—'Great cry and little wool.' I never fired one of them but once, and that was at the battle of the Salado, near San Antonio.

"During the fight, I came across a dead Mexican with one in his hands, and as my rifle was empty at the time, I hastily caught it up, placed the breech against my shoulder, as I was in the habit of doing with my own gun, and fired at a party of the enemy who were retreating from the field. My first impression was that I had been struck with a nine-pound cannon-ball. It kicked me heels over head, and I suppose kept on kicking me after I was down, for when I came to I found that my nose was unjointed and two of my ribs stove in. I have since found that Mexicans never place them to the shoulder, but hold them with both hands above their heads and fire at random, which accounts in great measure for the little execution done by them." (Sowell *Big Foot* 177-178) This story is an example of Bigfoot's humor, and his description of how the Mexican soldiers fired their guns is an example of how unimportant truth was when he could make a good story.

typical Texan exaggeration, was said to equal a thousand men. As soon as the bullets began to whistle, he seemed to grow taller and look grander, appearing "as unconcerned as if he had been out cornshucking."[7]

A company of Mexican cavalry charged, but their horses were startled by the gunshots. Some lost their riders, galloped back in confusion, and knocked down their own soldiers. The unhorsed cavalrymen could barely run in their large Mexican spurs. They tried to run on their toes so as to lift their big spurs from the ground, but after the battle, the earth looked like it had been gone over with a garden rake.

The Mexican cavalry dashed back out of range. When some Mexican horsemen stopped on a hill some distance up the creek, Green McCoy noticed them. He asked Andrew Sowell to come with him to the creek. They planned to tie their horses, slip within rifle shot of the cavalry, get a good shot each, and fall back to their horses.

The young men followed this plan. They tied their horses to a mesquite tree, bent low, and started to slip toward the cavalry, but they had taken only a few steps when they were startled by a low keen whistle near them. They looked around and saw a company of Mexican infantry no more than fifty paces away. The Mexicans, who had been hidden in the high grass, rose up and whistled the way a hunter whistles to a deer so it will stop and he can shoot it.

McCoy and Sowell sprang toward their horses. The Mexicans fired. Bark and mesquite beans fell on the volunteers' hats, but neither was touched. The terrified horses reared and plunged. McCoy and Sowell drew their knives, cut the horses' ropes, and leaped astride. They dashed off, bent low in their saddles. Sowell looked back. Some of the Mexicans were so near that he could see half way down the barrels of the big-mouthed *escopetas*. Musket balls cut the air, but Sowell and McCoy made it to camp. They were just in time to help their comrades drive back another Mexican charge.

The Mexican troops had been given mescal, a strong, intoxicating drink. Under its influence, they charged ahead, yelling like demons, throwing their hats, and shooting their *escopetas* in the very faces of Caldwell's men. Since the Texans had the protection of the high river banks, the Mexicans could not hold out for long against their fire. They had to retreat.

CHAPTER 4

The Dawson Massacre

The Texan strategy had been successful; the taunting expedition had worked. The Mexicans lost at least sixty men in the fight at Salado Creek; the Texans lost only one. But across the prairie came another group of Texans whose fate was to be quite different. The Mexicans noticed them riding toward the volunteers at Salado. It was the Dawson group—the Fayette County men who had started their journey fourteen hours ahead of the Hill family.

Mosby Dawson and his fifty-one volunteers had marched all the way from La Grange—about 150 miles—in only forty-eight hours. About fifteen miles west of Gonzales, they had come across yet another group of volunteers. The leader of that group was Jesse Billingsley, thirty-two, who had been wounded in the Battle of San Jacinto. He was a man of integrity and judgment, both public servant and tough *hombre*. He served as Representative in the First Congress of the Republic of Texas. In that office, he "furnished his own grub, slept on his own blanket, and wore a buckskin suit that he took from a Comanche Indian he killed in battle."[1] Billingsley tried to persuade Dawson to wait a couple of hours until all Billingsley's men arrived and until James S. Mayfield also arrived with his volunteer troops. Then the combined forces could travel together.

Dawson refused this sensible plan. He said he didn't want to "miss the fun."[2] The Dawson group rode through the night without even pausing to make camp. Both the men and the horses were worn out.

Alsey S. Miller, who had joined the company on the road and who had the only nearly fresh horse, went ahead as a scout. He reported that a battle was going on at the Salado Creek. The exhausted Dawson men had to decide whether to advance and try to join Caldwell in his fight or whether to retreat. They turned to old Zadock Woods for advice. Woods had more years than sense. He said that they had marched a long way to meet the Mexicans and declared, "I had rather die than retreat."[3]

Norman Woods did not agree with his father's plan. He saw that two Mexican units of about 600 men were moving toward their force of fifty-one. He urged retreat, but Mosby Dawson drew his pistol and said, "I'll shoot the first man who runs."[4]

The Texans looked around for some protection, but found only a grove of small mesquite trees.[5] It wasn't much, but it was all they had. The Mexicans pointed a cannon into the grove and stood ready to attack. Then they offered Mosby Dawson terms of surrender. He rejected the offer, and the battle was on. The Texans held the Mexicans back for a while, but they couldn't stand for long. Shots from the cannon ripped through the trees and struck them right and left.

Finally, even Dawson knew they could not win. It was surrender or die. Wounded, he came out of the thicket with a blanket on his rifle; it was the nearest thing he had to a white flag.

The Mexicans stopped firing.

But in spite of Dawson's flag, his own men fired. The Mexicans, seeing that the make-shift flag didn't seem to mean surrender after all, returned fire. Dawson fell.

Mexican cavalrymen leaped from their horses and dashed into the mesquite grove, their swords drawn. Texans and Mexicans struggled hand-to-hand. Joe Griffin seemed as strong as Hercules. Fighting furiously, he refused to surrender. When the stock of his gun broke, he jerked the limb off a mesquite tree and kept fighting, using the branch as a club until he was killed.[6]

Zadock Woods fell to the ground in an artillery barrage while he was reloading his gun. Norman ran to his side and caught a bullet in his hip as he bent over his father's body. Gonzalvo's horse was shot out from under him. He crawled over to his father and brother, intent on surrendering and taking care of them, but Norman handed him a pistol and told him to get away if he could. As Gonzalvo rose from the ground, a mounted Mexican soldier rushed at him with a lance. Gonzalvo grabbed the lance, jerked the Mexican soldier to the ground, leaped on his horse, and headed for home.[7] He rode until his horse broke down, then abandoned him and continued on foot.[8]

Young John Wilson was stationed at the crossing of Nash's Creek to warn anyone who came along about what was happening at San Antonio and the Salado Creek. The wounded Gonzalvo Woods made it to Nash's Creek and Wilson found him. He washed the blood from Gonzalvo's head and dressed his wounds with a thick paste of mashed prickly pear. Then he took him back to La Grange.[9]

Alsey Miller also escaped. He donned a Mexican sombrero, grabbed a fallen cavalryman's horse, and galloped across the prairie and all the way to Seguin.

The Mexicans hacked and stabbed their way among the fallen Texans. Colonel Carrasco stopped the bloodbath, exclaiming, "Such men are too brave to die!"[10]

Allen Morrell, the preacher Zenos Morrell's son, surrendered, but two Mexicans continued to attack him. One of the Mexicans hurled his lance. Allen leaped aside, but the lance grazed his left arm. He looked for shelter and dodged behind Colonel Carrasco's horse. The Mexican colonel drew his sword and drove his own soldiers away.[11] Thus, Allen Morrell survived. Because of Colonel Carrasco's efforts, the Mexicans spared the lives of fifteen captured Texans, but thirty-six lay fallen. The fight at the small grove near the Salado Creek had lasted less than an hour.

Victorious Mexicans stripped the dead for spoils. Norman Woods, who before the battle had wisely advised retreat, now lay among the Texan bodies. He was still alive, but his hip was shattered, and his body bled from five sword wounds. Instead of killing Norman Woods or leaving him to die, the Mexicans put him in an ox cart and took him with them.[12]

The Texas volunteers at the Salado had heard the roar of cannons and rifles. They understood that the battle must be between the Mexican forces and some other volunteers who were on their way to join them, but before the Texans at the Salado Creek could go to the Dawson group's assistance, the firing stopped.

The Aftermath

The Texans at the Salado Creek could see General Woll standing on his cannon, giving a victory speech. They were afraid that the defeated Texans were their friends and relatives. Later that night, they learned that what they feared was true, and Zenos Morrell got the dreadful news that his son, Allen, was in the Dawson group.[13]

The next morning, September 18, 1842, at daybreak in a heavy rain, Morrell and three other volunteers went to the battle ground. What they found there was so horrible that two of the men could not bear the sight and rode away. Mexican soldiers and horses lay dead all over the prairie, and

---

Norman Woods

Seven months later, on July 5, 1843, Norman Woods wrote his brother Gonzalvo from Molino del Rey, "I was shot across the hip at the time that captain Dawson ran out with the white flagg it was Corascoes order for his soldiers to disarm us and put us to death. We were released from this by an order from Genl Woll I was left on the ground as dead until they come to stripping us and tearing the clothes off of me. I had recovered enough to ask for quarters which was granted by a sargent who kept off the soldiers with his sword. I had received five wounds with the sword four on the head and one in the left side which nearly proved fatal." (Letters of the 'Dawson Men'" *SWHQ* 38, 257-260)

scattered among the little cluster of bushes lay thirty-five Texans, some with their heads cut off, some with their arms and legs cut off. The rain had washed the bodies clean of blood and grime, and they lay like marble statues. Zadock Woods lay among them, his flowing white hair disheveled.[14]

Some of the bodies were so cut up, Morrell couldn't tell who they were. Frantic with fear for his son, he examined the dead men's feet searching for a scar that Allen had had since childhood, but he found no such scar.

Morrell wrote down the names of all the men he recognized so he could tell their families.[15] He and the other volunteers had buried a single soldier earlier, digging the grave with their Bowie knives.[16] But thirty-five bodies were too many to bury that way, and since they had no hoes or spades, they had to leave their dead comrades lying on the open prairie.

The same day Morrell was cataloging the dead and searching for his son, Billingsley, Mayfield, and their volunteers joined Mathew Caldwell's men at Salado Creek. Many called Billingsley and Mayfield cowards for not joining the Dawson group.

September 17, 1842 had brought both victory and defeat — the victory at Salado Creek and the defeat of the Dawson men. The Texans were stunned by the Dawson massacre and set out after General Woll, who left San Antonio two days later.

Zenos Morrell went into San Antonio in search of news about his son, Allen. The Tejana woman who had warned General Woll about the Texans saw Morrell and told him she had watched the prisoners as the Mexican soldiers marched them up the street. "Your son was with them; he had his coat off and was all bloody."[17]

Now Morrell knew that his son, whom he described as "a mere boy," was alive, but was a captive. A Mrs. Elliot, who Morrell refers to as the English foreign minister's wife, had a list of all the prisoners' names. She, too, had seen Allen Morrell. She told Zenos that although Allen was wounded in the shoulder, the injury was not serious. She also told him that Allen was no longer without a coat. She had taken a green blanket-coat from her own son and had put it on Allen. He later said that the coat saved his life.[18]

Morrell caught up with the Texans who were pursuing the Mexicans. On September 19, two days after the Battle of Salado Creek and the Dawson fight, the Texans neared General Woll's rear-guard at the Hondo River.

Ranger Captain Jack Hays wanted to follow the Mexicans and capture their cannon, but he didn't have enough men. General Mayfield made a speech calling for volunteers to join Hays, but the men did not respond. Morrell said Mayfield's "was the voice of a stranger."[19] Frightened for his son, Morrell himself galloped through the volunteer camp, his old fur hat in his hand, urging the men to join Hays: "Boys, you have come out here one to two hundred miles from home to hunt the elephant. He has been running from you for two days. We have got him in close quarters, just up on that hill. . . . The old fellow can't hurl his missiles of death at us more than two or three times before we will stop his breath."[20]

The men listened to Morrell. More than were needed got ready for the attack.

Cowards?

There are reports that volunteers under James S. Mayfield and Jesse Billingsley, who had tried to persuade Dawson to wait for him, came within view of the battle while it was raging. These reports said that Mayfield and Billingsley gave orders not to go to the Dawson men's aid, but instead, stayed in the distance while their fellow Texans were massacred. However, Rufus Perry, who was with the group, reported that he, Sam Walker, a man named Flint, and a "Tonkaway" Indian were ordered to go ahead of the others to see what was happening. They saw the battleground from the top of a hill, saw Dawson raise the flag, and saw Alsey Miller gallop away. They shouted at him, but he later said he believed them to be Indians and did not respond. According to Rufus Perry, Billingsley and Mayfield were at least three miles from the battleground at the time and had no idea what had happened until he reported to them. If Perry's report is correct, the Billingsley and Mayfield men could not have reached Dawson's force in time to be of help, and would surely have been slaughtered had they tried. (Weyand and Wade 152, 157)

CHAPTER 5

Disgrace at the Hondo

Jack Hays and Old Paint Caldwell led the attack against the Mexican army at the Hondo River on September 19, 1842. Captain Hays told his men they were going to attack and that the volunteer troops in the rear would support them. The Rangers "collected around their gallant captain to make this desperate charge."[1] Hays led the way, and the Rangers followed, firing as they went and ignoring the grapeshot raking them as they rode among the cannons. The fight was lively for the Rangers, but the volunteers lagged behind.

Musket balls whistled all around. Captain Jack Hays' horse bounded sharply. It was hit.

Nick Wren's horse was also hit. Nick fell to the ground.

Bigfoot Wallace's mule bounded forward, braying at every jump.[2] He pulled the reins hard, but the mule charged on. Then a musket ball burned the end of its nose; it wheeled and galloped the other way. Bigfoot lay low on the mule's neck, firing as he went.[3]

Enemy soldiers at the cannons either fled or were killed. Some hid under the cannons to shield themselves from the Rangers. Kit Ackland leaned low from his saddle, pistol in hand, and shot between the spokes of the cannon wheels.[4]

Captain Jack Hays and Ranger Sam Luckey were riding together. Woll had offered five hundred dollars for Captain Hays' head. Luckey's horse was finer looking than the one Hays' was now riding, which caused a Mexican soldier to mistake Luckey for Hays. The soldier took careful aim and shot Luckey. The ball went under Luckey's right shoulder blade and came out just below the left nipple, barely missing the heart.[5] Ben Highsmith was near and caught Luckey as he fell from his horse which galloped away. Luckey cried out for water, and Highsmith gave him a drink.

Later, Ben Highsmith stopped his horse under a mesquite tree. A cannon ball cut off the top of the tree. Mesquite limbs dangled off horse and rider as Highsmith's horse ran wild.

The Rangers spurred their horses among the cannon, yelling for the volunteers to help. The volunteers did not answer. The Rangers captured both cannons, but without the volunteers, they were forced to retreat.

The Texan volunteers stood only a few hundred yards from the battle. The 200 men watched and did nothing.

Maverick and the other captives watched, too—from the Mexican side, helpless prisoners. Maverick later said that a charge by the Texan volunteers would have saved the day, but without them Hays was forced back out of the range of Mexican gunfire. Maverick and the other captives had to march westward with Woll and his army, and Hays had to watch them go.[6]

Why Didn't the Volunteers Help?

During the fight, the Texan volunteers had stood uselessly in their ranks, maddened by thirst, delay, and lack of harmony among their leaders.[7] Highsmith thought their

---

Lucky Luckey

This kind of wound was familiar to the well-named Luckey. It was exactly the opposite of one he had received the year before in an Indian fight at Bandera Pass. In that battle, he was shot under the left shoulder blade and the ball came out below the right nipple (Sowell *Early Settlers* 26). Ben Highsmith was with Luckey on that occasion as well and gave him water then, too. Luckey survived both wounds and later became a member of the Senate of the Republic.

shocking behavior was because of a misunderstanding as to who would command the charge. Ben McCulloch thought it was because Old Paint Caldwell listened to popular opinion rather than leading in his usual aggressive way.[8]

Some historians blame the failure at Hondo on the Texans' character and lack of training. They say that the Texans, though brave to the point of foolhardiness and though marvelous as single fighters, were a poor excuse for an army. They didn't have the slightest idea what team work was; every man thought for himself and fought for himself.

Indeed, these volunteers were a loosely organized group of individual fighters who were held together by a peculiar mixture of idealism, war fever, and individual commitment. This was sometimes admirable—and often inefficient. They were not used to taking orders. As volunteers, they elected their leaders, and those who had the most military experience

---

Morrell's Account

There are several accounts of what happened at the Hondo River. Most of them tell much the same story, but Zenos Morrell's account is quite different. His eagerness to save his young son, Allen, may have influenced his view.

Morrell's account of the Hondo River Battle describes the men as so eager to fight that not a single one would even volunteer to stay behind to care for a wounded Ranger. Someone had to be commanded to do so. Morrell describes the Texan volunteers as standing in good order, facing the Mexican cannon, and firing on command. He describes the Mexican cannon shooting over the Texans' heads and missing them, while every Mexican who manned the cannon was killed by Texan fire. According to Morrell, only one Texan was wounded, and only one horse killed. He also says that when night fell, the volunteers were eager to continue the fight, but Ranger Ben McCulloch advised that the attack be postponed until morning.

Morrell says that during the night Woll moved some six miles away, and when morning came, General Mayfield "commenced a harangue" doubting the wisdom of the going after them. This demoralized the men. They scattered, and many returned home. He blamed Mayfield for discouraging the expedition. At last, Morrell also gave up, and went home, heartbroken for his lost son. (Morrell 176)

were not always chosen. Decisions were reached by consensus or by vote.

Democracy and individual independence are less than ideal qualities for a small, poorly equipped force of guerilla fighters facing a large and organized army. On several occasions the Texans paused for debate, and disaster resulted.

The battle at the Hondo River is a mark of shame for Texas. Mexican Colonel Carrasco commented that the Texans who fought at the Hondo River "were not fit to stand in the shoes of those who fought at the Salado."[9] This is ironic since many were the same men.

Old Paint Caldwell was blamed for the Texan failure. He limped home in disgrace. Humiliated and outraged, he sank into depression and illness. He died three months later.

The Dawson Massacre and the Disgrace at the Hondo were only the first of many mistakes and sufferings for the Texans. The failure to free the captured Texans at Hondo was disastrous. Now the captives would be taken to an unknown location somewhere in Mexico and guarded by a force of unknown size. Now an attempt to free them would mean mounting an invasion—or using diplomacy. And diplomacy was foreign to the Texan volunteers.

CHAPTER 6
San Antonio Captives

After the Hondo fight, the prisoners captured in San Antonio were marched west into Mexico to a place called San Fernando de Rosas. On October 4, ten of the fifteen men who had escaped being killed in the Dawson fight also arrived. They were placed in a separate prison and were not allowed to visit the men who had been taken in San Antonio. However, a Dawson man, John Bradley, managed to get a note to the San Antonio captives telling them about the massacre. From that note, Sam Maverick learned that Joe Griffin had been coming to try to help him and had died heroically in the Dawson fight.

Maverick wrote in his journal: "God knows I feel his death as the hardest piece of fortune we have suffered in Texas." He continued, addressing Griffin directly: "I mourn thee as a true and faithful friend and a brother."[1]

The San Antonio prisoners petitioned Governor Francisco Mejia of Nuevo León for clothes to be given the Dawson men, who had been stripped on the battlefield and were almost naked. Mejia ignored the request, but some U.S. citizens who were in Mexico gave the Texans supplies for their long march.

The Texan captives had to cross deserts and mountains. They were often denied water for long periods of time, then were allowed to drink only after the water had been muddied by the guards' horses. They endured ridicule and had to sleep in manure-filled sheep pens and on bloody rocks where cattle had been slaughtered. Maverick writes matter-of-factly about camping in "cow dung a foot thick" and about damp quarters "which appeared to be used as a privy."[2]

The intelligent and adventurous Maverick found things to interest him in spite of the hardships. He noticed which areas were good for agriculture and which had good grazing. He managed to inquire about the price of land. He enjoyed the mountain views. His diary shows that he had an amazing ability to enjoy life and an intense interest in land even in such severe circumstances.

Some of the Mexican people they met on the road were abusive, but others extended kindness. When they were in San Fernando de Agua Verde, Marina Rodrigues y Taylor sent Maverick and four other prisoners three meals a day each of the eight days they were there. At another place where the prisoners camped, a little boy brought them fruit every day hidden inside his shirt.[3]

Life wasn't entirely dreary. The captive Texans sometimes had a bit of fun with the Mexicans. Once William Trimble and a Mexican soldier began to dance, outdoing each other in speed and complexity. A crowd of Americans and Mexicans were watching. When Trimble realized that he was about to be beaten, he suddenly stopped dancing, clapped his hands, and crowed like a rooster. Then he began talking fast. The Mexican was so startled, he left the dancing circle. A Texan captive commented, "The way the Mexican outdid us afforded great mirth to the bystanders."[4]

CHAPTER 7

The Republic of Texas Challenges Mexico

Over President Sam Houston's objections, the Texas Congress passed a bill that authorized the annexation of all Mexican territory north of the Rio Grande along with part of the Mexican states of Coahuila, Tamaulipas, Durango, and Sinaloa. In other words, the Texas Congress laid claim to two-thirds of Mexico—an area larger than the entire United States of that day.

Texas was weak, penniless, and in chaos. It could not possibly succeed at such a land grab. It had only 395 rifles and 581 barrels of gun powder. There was no standing army and no money to finance a war. The Republic of Texas was seven million dollars in debt and was not able to get loans. It had plenty of land that might have been sold to raise money, but there weren't buyers for the land. Moreover, Texas had problems keeping peace inside the Republic itself. Angry Indian tribes threatened settlers, and bandit gangs fought for control in Northeast Texas. The conflicts were so serious they could be called civil war. The Republic could not defeat the enemies within its own borders; it could not reasonably expect to defeat an armed nation.

Sam Houston understood this, but Texans wouldn't listen to reason. They had absolute faith in their fighting abilities and in the superiority of the Anglo-Saxon race. They were so blinded by war fever and racism that to even consider the possibility of defeat was thought cowardly.

Houston did all he could to discourage the attempt to invade Mexico. He knew that an attempt to free Maverick and the other San Antonio captives by force was doomed to fail. Diplomatic strategies would be more effective. However, he had to think about public opinion in both Texas and Mexico. Texans wanted war, and Mexico was watching closely. If Texas fought, men would die in a lost cause, and Texas might even lose the independence it had won at San Jacinto. However, if Houston publicly opposed the expedition, Mexico would think that Texas was weak, and that could cause more attacks. Since Houston could not prevent the invasion, he decided to take charge of it, at least enough to prevent the Texas hotheads from being treated as outlaws and pirates.[1] The endorsement of the Texas government gave some protection to any Texans who might be captured. Houston was in the awkward position of both trying to avoid war and also trying to take care of the foolish Texans.

Houston decided on a strategy of delay. He waited until October to appoint a general. He chose General Alexander Somervell, forty-six. When Houston talked to Somervell, he emphasized the problems the expedition faced and may also have discussed the strategy of delay. But when he spoke to the public, he sounded a different note. He referred to the "God of armies," and said, "ere the banner of Mexico shall triumphantly float upon the banks of the Sabine, the Texian standard of the single star . . . shall display its bright folds in Liberty's triumph . . . ."[2]

Eager for action, the Texan volunteers waited outside San Antonio. The delay was as unreasonably long as the call to arms had been unreasonably hasty. Anglo volunteers, Pro-Texas Indians, and Texas Rangers all stood waiting for orders and for ammunition. The government sent only a few munitions, and that few were stolen en route.

Somervell took his good easy time in assuming the position of leader of the expedition to rescue Maverick and the other San Antonio captives. He did not even show up at the camp in San Antonio until November 4, and in spite of the already long delay, he ordered the troops to wait for a cannon to arrive from Gonzales.

In the meantime, Houston sent Somervell a series of confusing messages. He told Somervell not to engage the enemy and not to cross the border unless he was sure he could win.[3] He told him not to seize supplies, but didn't send any money to buy them. Things were a muddle, spirits were sinking, and Somervell waited for the cannon.

CHAPTER 8

At the Camp

John Christopher Columbus Hill along with his father, Asa, and his brother, Jeffrey, arrived at the camp outside San Antonio too late for the victorious battle at Salado Creek, too late for the horrific Dawson Massacre, and too late to be part of the disgrace at Hondo. The early events had been breathlessly quick. The San Antonio men were captured on September 11, 1842, and in less than ten days, Rangers and volunteers were in battle. But now things froze to a shivering standstill.

Winter came early in 1842, and the weather was cold and wet. There had been a summer drought that caused crop failure, but the autumn weather changed sharply. The rivers swelled and the land lay under water. By mid November, the rains became torrents. The men sheltered their precious ammunition under small tents made of blankets or stretched beef hides while they themselves faced the elements unprotected and wretched.

They were hungry as well as cold and wet. There were no vegetables or bread. They had only meat they hunted or "borrowed."[1] As the wait grew long and suffering increased, they began to quarrel with each other. Some of them wouldn't share meat even if they had more than enough. When Captain Bogart's men killed a bear said to weigh three hundred pounds, men from other companies only got to smell the barbecue; they had to eat acorns.[2]

But that was not the worst. Some of the volunteers stole blankets from citizens in San Antonio; some chased people out of their homes and took the homes for themselves. Others got drunk and went on a ransacking, plundering rampage. They even sacked the home of the legendary hero Deaf Smith's widow. And rape was not unknown. Some volunteers were so wild that General Somervell feared an uprising and revolt.

All this was hard to bear for the high-minded among the Texas volunteers. Even the most idealistic among them must have seen that many of their group were hoodlums.

The Texas government at Washington-on-the-Brazos heard of the volunteers' criminal acts and sent reprimands. The weak young Republic could not enforce a stronger punishment.

At the camp, 1,250 volunteers waited in the cold and rain, ready to fight a hungry, threadbare war. Time passed. The men grew more and more discouraged. They had no clear idea of when or whether the expedition would get underway. At last, 500 of them called it quits and went home. But 750 stuck it out. No one made them stay. It was a free, if miserable, choice.

Why Did the Texans Stay at the Camp?

One reason the Texans stayed at the camp is that they suffered from war fever. Their heads were full of dreams of conquest, and they yearned for battle. They could not see reality; they could see only their dreams, and they were willing to endure winter rains without shelter in order to be part of the Texan cause.

A related reason was the desire for honor and glory. It would seem that physical discomfort and low companions would discourage dreams of grand deeds, but dreams outweigh simple truth. Boys in buckskin were ready to go to their graves remembering the Alamo, and they would wait in the rain for the chance.

A more earthy reason volunteers stayed was to get revenge. Throughout Texas, unrighted wrongs abounded, and Texans wanted to avenge them. Bigfoot Wallace had lost a brother and a cousin at Goliad, and true to the values of his Scottish ancestor, William Wallace, Bigfoot was after revenge.

Some volunteers stayed at the camp because they believed their aggression would bring peace. Many settlers had been forced to flee the area because of Mexican raids. Farmers felt that fighting back against Mexican wrongs was the only answer. "Our homes are endangered; our property has been pillaged. Our people have been murdered, and there is no peace, no security left for us, unless we carry the war into the enemy's land."[3]

The Texas economy was at a low point and had been for several years. Poverty was a serious problem. Some men were simply out of work and had nothing better to do than

Goliad

The Goliad Massacre on Palm Sunday, March 27, 1836, is one of the most dreadful events in the Texas Revolution. James W. Fannin surrendered after obtaining General Urrea's agreement to written terms of surrender. The main points were that Fannin and his men would be treated as prisoners of war according to the practices of civilized nations. They were to be sent to the United States. General Urrea knew that according to the Mexican law, all foreigners who took up arms against the government were to be shot. But Urrea also knew that if he refused the Texan's terms, they would fight on. Although they had 500 spare muskets and nine brass cannons, the Texans could not have won. However, they would have killed many Mexican soldiers before they were defeated. Therefore, Urrea deceived them and said they would be freed. Fannin was even deceived by being taken to locate a ship for the Texans' return home. The Texans were told they would be put to work and then released. They were divided into three groups and marched in different directions. Then they were shot at close range. The wounded, who had not marched out to work, were executed in the presidio. Twenty-eight Texans escaped, including John C. Duval, later biographer of Bigfoot Wallace. Twenty were spared, probably because they had needed skills, but 342 men were killed. Their bodies were piled together and burned. The remains were left exposed at Goliad.

stay with the volunteers. Others had a clear and ignoble goal: they were out for plunder. Worse still were the scoundrels drawn to the cause by lust for blood.

Bigfoot Wallace described the volunteers as, "a motley, mixed-up crowd . . . that somehow had got on the wrong side of the fence and been left out in the cold; renegades and refugees from justice . . . ready for anything or any enterprise that afforded a reasonable prospect of excitement and plunder. Dare-devils they were all, and afraid of nothing under the sun except a due bill."[4]

In this motley crew was young John Christopher Columbus Hill trying to do his duty to God and his country and to keep his promise to take care of his father and brother.

Fortunately, there were more high minded men than scoundrels, and among them were personalities colorful enough to combat boredom. One of the most high-minded was John Day Morgan. He had suffered on the Santa Fe trail and had recently been released from prison in Mexico City. The terms of his release included never again taking up arms against Mexico. If he were caught, it meant certain death. Yet he was so devoted to the Texan cause that he had hardly reached home when he joined the volunteers, ready to risk all. He called himself John Day rather than his true name of John Morgan since that name was on the Mexican death list. But the name change must not have helped much since the prisoners then called him John Day Morgan.

Tender-hearted Morgan was born in England, as were several other volunteers. There were also men from Canada, Scotland, Ireland, Austria, Germany, and eighteen different states of the U.S.A. The men had grown up in many different cultures and spoke in many accents, but their differences were smaller than the things they had in common. The idea that true manhood involved bravery and bravado was common to all, as was the hunger for adventure and conquest.

Big Ewen Cameron, thirty-four, was one of the most colorful personalities. He spoke in a Scottish Highland brogue, and his friendly ways made him a favorite. A natural leader, he and his "cowboys" were famous as raiders and fighters on the Mexican border. People of our day might think of Cameron as simply a cattle thief, but he came from the culture of Scottish border raiders—a kind of cattle thief honored by tradition and by the habits of generations. Among Cameron's cowboys was cheerful little Henry Whaling, a fearless fighter with personality to spare. The bits that we know about Henry Whaling make us wish for more.

Most of the volunteers were young. Those as old as seventeen were considered men, but John C. C. Hill, although only thirteen and the youngest, was not the only volunteer under seventeen. The others were Gilbert Brush, whose background is unknown; Harvey Sellers, who had joined the volunteers without the consent of his mother and without thinking that she might need him; Orlando Phelps, the tall, fair son of jovial Dr. Phelps; Billy Reese, younger brother of Captain Charles Reese; and Jessie Yocum, who probably joined the volunteers because he had no place to go. His family, accused of crimes by their neighbors, had all been driven from the area or killed.[5]

These youngsters became good friends, and stuck together. Their enthusiasm and their dead-eye accuracy as sharp shooters earned them the title *the fire eaters*.

CHAPTER 9

On the Trail–Bog, Drought, Flood, and Stampede

At last, on November 23, the men at the Salado broke camp and started the march to Mexico. Following the soldiers were 300 cattle, 200 pack mules, and the cannon. Six miles outside of San Antonio, Somervell decided that the cannon was too heavy for the journey and sent it back. It had served only to delay them.

The Texans hooted with scornful laughter. They had waited three miserable weeks for that cannon to arrive. Just the same, they were happy to be on their way. One of them wrote that the men had "high spirits and bright anticipations" and were "... proudly looking forward to the time when, face to face we should meet our country's foe, and hurl his haughty insolence back to his teeth!"[1]

Those high expectations soon sank in the mud. The men had expected to make a bee-line for Laredo, heading south on the well-worn Laredo Trail. Instead, Somervell led the troops west toward Presidio. He said he wanted to confuse Mexican spies. He succeeded in doing that, but he confused himself and his men as well. It had begun raining shortly after they began the march, and it rained for three days. To make matters worse, they got lost in the Atascosa bog.[2]

Cattle, horses, mules, and men sank in the boggy soil. Sometimes the men had to roll a horse over and over until they got him to a place where the earth would bear his weight. Then he might make only a few steps until he sank again. Abandoned skillets, blankets, and saddle bags littered the wet land.

Bigfoot Wallace's mule sank in the bog. Some of the men pushed on his rump and while others tugged at his head. At last, with a heave, the big mule lurched out. John C. C. Hill's lively, expressive pony, Jim Dandy, sank in the bog, too. He looked hopeless and held perfectly still until John C. C. and his brother, Jeffrey, got him out. Many others were not so lucky.

The line of volunteers stretched about a mile in length and twisted into fantastic curves: men, mules, and horses, floundered, half submerged. Pack mules and horses that were hopelessly stuck in the bog had to be shot to keep them from suffering slow and lingering deaths.[3] Now much needed horses were scarcer than ever.

When the weary Texans finally got through the bog, they faced miles of South Texas chaparral bushes and tall grass.

No Man's Land

Historically the Nueces River had been the Southern boundary of Texas. In 1836 Texas passed a law declaring that the Rio Grande was the Southern boundary. The disputed land between the Nueces and Rio Grande rivers became a no-man's land. Neither country could maintain effective control. Cattle thieves from Texas, the "cowboys," rationalized their thefts by saying the Mexican army had carried off Texans' cattle without paying for them. Criminals and cutthroats from both countries ranged in the disputed area. Each country accused the other country of helping the outlaws; neither was successful in controlling them.

The brush was hard to ride through and the grass was hard for the animals to eat. It was so dry they could barely stay alive on it. The little water they could find was dirty and sour. Both horses and men suffered from thirst.

The men didn't have much more to eat than the horses did—just corn meal and a little beef. A few of the soldiers found some unfamiliar plants that had big roots. They dug them up for supper. They were happy to have found a vegetable for their diet because they suffered from scurvy, an illness caused from lack of vitamins. The cooked roots tasted something like potatoes, but the mild tasting plant soon made them sick.

On December 2, 1842, the Texans moved from drought to flood. The Nueces River, normally only a thin stream, was now high, wide, and impossible to cross. With considerable backwoods genius, the men cut down tall trees that grew along the banks and in three days constructed a bridge.[4]

After crossing the river, the men pitched camp and butchered the last of the cattle—the 300 they had started the journey with were gone before they even reached the border. They were far from home and without a supply of food. But they had made it through the bog and across the river, and they were alive. That was cause for celebration, and they recited poetry around the camp fire.

The exhausted men decided to take a couple of days to rest. A few men on horseback kept guard at night. The pack mules and horses were free to graze. On the second night, the guards noticed that the animals were jittery. To calm the herd, the guards whistled and sang as they circled on their mounts. Later they realized that the animals were sensing a change of weather that took the men by surprise. A sudden thunderstorm struck. The bright flashes of lightning and the great claps of thunder frightened the mules and horses. The animals ran over the sleeping men, who came close to dying under the hooves of their own horses. The guards galloped beside the panicked herd until they were calm enough to be led back into camp.

On the Trail—Bog, Drought, Flood, and Stampede 47

Still exhausted, the Texans resumed their march with Captain Jack Hays in the lead. In order to see that no prowling bands of Indians or Mexican bandits made a sudden attack, he would sometimes ride as much as a day ahead of the group. Ranger Ben McCulloch, Flacco, and two other Lipan Apaches rode with him.[5]

Exhausted

The Texans were worn out by the long months in the cold camp, and by the long, difficult trail. Several of them told stories about exhausted sleep. Bigfoot Wallace, John Day Morgan, and S. B. Hendricks were among them.

Bigfoot Wallace

Bigfoot Wallace had the job of guarding a scout the Texans caught as they marched toward Laredo. Bigfoot determined not to let his prisoner escape, so when night fell, he used him as a pillow. But Bigfoot was so tired, he didn't even notice when the prisoner slipped out from under his head, slipped a saddle into his place, and sneaked away. Now they couldn't surprise the enemy. Bigfoot was mortified. His deep sleep had endangered the expedition. (Duval 56)

John Day Morgan

When the volunteers reached the Rio Grande a few miles from Laredo, they reined in their horses and paused to decide their next move. It was late evening, and John Day Morgan fell into a deep sleep with his bridle in his hand. When he awoke, he found himself alone. Not one of his comrades had missed him as they moved on in the darkness. Morgan listened for some echo from the advancing army, but he heard nothing. He decided that the best thing to do was to give the horse its head. The horse struck out in a trot. Neighing all the way, he went straight to the army. (Jenkins 132)

S. B. Hendricks

Hendricks recorded that he had not slept for five nights but at last seized his chance while another sentinel kept watch outside Laredo. He was so tired that "a diabolical wolf had the audacity to run over me . . . and I was not even awakened." (Hendricks 127)

CHAPTER 10

Laredo

Bigfoot Wallace led an advance party into Laredo. Instead of Mexican troops, armed and ready to fight, they saw the women of the town going about their ordinary tasks. Not a soldier was in sight. The Mexican soldiers that had been staying there had left. At daybreak, more volunteers went into the city. John Day Morgan stopped at a private house. The woman of the house cheerfully gave him breakfast. She told him she was worried about having Texan troops in the town. Morgan assured her that Texas soldiers were too honorable to disturb women and children. Then he thanked her, returned to camp, and rested.

Considering that there were obvious hoodlums among the Texas volunteers, it is hard to understand why John Day Morgan would give the woman such assurance. Apparently he believed his ideal vision of Texans rather than the truth before his eyes. His own kindly, idealistic nature may have clouded his view.

With great politeness Don Florencio Villareal, Alcalde of Laredo, formally surrendered the city to General Somervell. One elderly member of Villareal's delegation, after shaking hands with several of the Texan officers, courteously extended his hand to Flacco. The Indian sternly drew himself up and leveled his spear at the old gentleman. He made it clear that he would rather kill him on the spot than greet him as a friend. Flacco would not speak to a single Mexican and "appeared to be constantly watching for an opportunity to avenge the blood of his countrymen."[1]

The Texans also wanted to fight, but when they went into Laredo, instead of a battle, they found a welcome. The women gave them cakes. This wasn't what they wanted even though they were out of food, and the cold weather made them need it badly. They were hungry for a fight.

Outrage at Laredo

By now, the Texan warriors were a sorry sight. All of them were dirty and tattered. Many were on foot carrying their baggage. Somervell demanded supplies from the town. All he got was a few sacks of flour and a dozen cattle, barely enough food for one day. The Texans were given no fresh horses, no clothing, and no blankets. They considered that being given so little was an insult.

The Texan scoundrels who had abused the people of San Antonio weren't any kinder to the people of Laredo. That rough group, about sixty men,[2] got drunk and looted the town. They ransacked stores from top to bottom. Groups of soldiers wandered through the streets breaking down doors that stood in their way. Three of them grabbed Alcalde Villareal. They put a rope around his neck and held a gun to his head threatening to kill him unless he gave them silver. Fortunately, Major Henry Davis came along and made them release Villareal. He was so disgusted with the men in his command, he resigned and went home.

When John Day Morgan woke from his nap at the camp, he returned to Laredo and found it sacked and robbed. The woman who had given him breakfast saw him and reminded him of what he had said about Texan soldiers being honorable. Morgan turned away from her, almost in tears.[3]

At last, the scoundrels left the terrorized town and went back to camp driving livestock ahead of them. They looked like dirty clowns. They had wrapped and tied all kinds of clothing and blankets around themselves. They had even taken nightgowns, baby clothes, and embroidered pillows.

Somervell had guards ready. They stopped the scoundrels and made them give up what they had taken. They put the stolen things in a big pile so the citizens could take what wasn't ruined.

Thomas Jefferson Green, forty, excused the conduct of the men and criticized Somervell for showing more concern for "poor Mexicans" than for his own men. All the older soldiers, especially the ones who had been prisoners and had known the kindness of Mexican women, were shocked and angry at such behavior. They looked down on the looters and ridiculed them. Many of the younger soldiers felt the same.[4] Joseph D. McCutchan, nineteen, wrote his feelings in his diary:

> Here was a town on the soil claimed by Texas; its inhabitants, claiming to be Texians, had opened their door to us, as to friends... and yet, those inhabitants were not safe in the possession of their private property. Suffice it to say, Texas must wear a stain for the conduct of a few disorderly volunteers.[5]

Charles Elliot, the British *chargé de affairs* in the Republic of Texas, called the looters "loafers—the dangerous and unprincipled set of people of which Sam Houston is so anxious to free the country."[6]

Somervell was afraid there would be more trouble if the soldiers stayed near Laredo, so he ordered the men to break camp.

Green

Thomas Jefferson Green came to Texas in 1836. He had attended West Point and was made brigadier general in the Texas army. However, he was sent to the United States to recruit volunteers and did not fight in any battles for the Republic of Texas. He was a great self-promoter. The evidence of his own writings and comments by people who knew him, show him to be swashbuckling and vain. He was also a skilled survivor who knew how to seize opportunity when it presented itself.

CHAPTER 11

Somervell Finale

On the Road Again

The Texans marched only a few miles along the riverbank when, to their astonishment, Somervell again led them away from a clear trail and into dense chaparral. He said Mexican forces were on their way, and rough country was a good place to conceal the men. He was right to think no one would expect men to go into such terrain. The prickly pear and thorn bushes were so thick, the men pulled their legs up and perched cross-legged on their suffering horses.

They stopped for the night in a mesquite flat where there was no grazing for the horses and no water for man or beast. General Somervell reprimanded the men for their lawless behavior in Laredo and asked that all who wanted to continue into Mexico gather on a nearby hill. Five hundred men went to that hill. One hundred and fifty did not; they had had enough of the cold and hunger on what seemed an endless and pointless expedition. They were released and started the long trek home.

Crossing the Rio Grande

Somervell decided to cross the Rio Grande at the village of Guerrero, about fifty-five miles south of Laredo and two miles from the Rio Grande. It was on the Salado Creek, at this point a deep stream that joined the Rio Grande. It should have taken the troops two days to reach Guerrero, but Somervell once more led them a winding way. It took the 500 Texans a week to get to the spot across from Guerrero where they were to ford the river.

General Thomas Jefferson Green wrote:

> This tardy and zigzag march completely bewildered the enemy, and they took for a cunning military manoeuvre what the tattered pantaloons and sore shins of our men too plainly told them was an unpardonable piece of stupidity and a cruel waste of time.[1]

However, in Laredo they had gotten 200 pounds of flour and divided it among the men. They also had taken a few beeves and had found sheep and good corn along the way, so by their standards they ate well for a few days.[2]

Somervell

Alexander Somervell's (1796-1852) record of service along with his background as a businessman, suggest that he could not have been the bumbling incompetent that the volunteers thought he was. Born in Maryland, he became a planter in Louisiana and a merchant in Missouri. He moved to Texas in 1833 and was granted land in Stephen F. Austin's second colony. He was cited for bravery in the "Grass Fight" against the Mexicans in 1835, fought in the battle of San Jacinto, and served as secretary of war for the Republic of Texas. He later served in the Texas Senate and as both land inspector and county clerk.

"It has been conjectured that President Houston never intended an aggressive movement against Mexico, and that Somervell acted under secret orders in disbanding his men. If the General had intended to make the expedition a failure, he could not have done it more effectually than he did." (Homer S. Thrall from Nance *Dare-devils 3*) In an affidavit some forty years later, George Lord said that he overheard Somervell telling Colonel Cook that Houston had ordered him to break up the expedition. Cook reportedly replied, "General, we cannot break up this expedition, the men will mutinize . . . My advice is to fling every impediment in its way and let it break itself up." (Nance *Attack* 497)

The fact that Somervell was given the position of Collector of Customs for the Port of Calhoun as a reward for leading the expedition lends additional weight to this interpretation.

When they got to the river, they found two canoes in the bushes on the river bank. The horses swam across. The canoes carried men and baggage. The process was slow — it took three hours to get seventy-five men across. They made camp near the river.

A freezing downpour drove some of the men to invite themselves into the huts of some Carrizo Indians, but there was no shelter for their horses. They froze to death where they were tied.

Somervell tried to requisition one hundred horses and supplies, but the citizens of Guerrero could offer them only some old hats and shoes and some soggy blankets. Jack Hays demanded $5,000 instead of supplies, but the frightened populace only had $381. That even intelligent Jack Hays thought the small farmers in the village of Guerrero had wealth shows how people can believe in a dream instead of in the truth that is right before their eyes. Nothing in those rural villages suggested wealth.

Re-Crossing the Rio Grande: The Somervell Expedition Ends

Somervell took the men back across the Rio Grande and said he thought they should go home. General Thomas Jefferson Green disagreed. "Does any glory fall on the general who marches his army up the hill and then back down again?"[3] he demanded. Nevertheless, Somervell decided to call it quits. On December 19, 1842, he announced that the expedition was over and that the army should march north to Gonzales to disband. Clearly he wanted to keep the men together for safety until they were nearer home.

To the men the decision was unexpected and unreasonable. What had they come for? Maverick and the other captured Texans were still in Mexican hands, and the Texans had not enriched themselves a cent. Even the honorable George B. Erath commented that he had hoped to get at least one good Spanish horse.[4] Moreover, they did not have enough provisions to make it home. Having just made the arduous trip to the border, they well knew the hardships that a return would involve, but they still had illusions about the wealth of Mexico.[5]

When General Somervell broke camp and started back, the men were outraged. The thought of having traveled so many miserable miles for no reason did not set well with their "belligerent spirits and dauntless hearts."[6] But 150 men turned back home. Thus, added to the 150 who had left earlier, Somervell's hard and discouraging winding way had spared considerable hardship, suffering, and possibly death to a total of 300 men.

CHAPTER 12

The Expedition Divides

Five of the eight company captains decided to continue the expedition. They included William S. Fisher, Ewen Cameron, and William Eastland, an old frontiersman and soldier. Three hundred three men stayed with them and elected William Fisher as their commander. Aggressive Thomas Jefferson Green seized the position of second in command. Asa Hill, Jeffrey Hill, John C. C. Hill, and all the fire eaters were among those who continued the expedition.

According to various sources, including Bigfoot Wallace and Orlando Phelps, Somervell gave the men who remained permission to "go down the river with General Fisher's command and fight the enemy wherever found."[1] To the group, this meant that the Republic of Texas legally authorized their invasion of Mexico.

A large majority of the Ranger company decided against staying with the venture. However, they stayed on four more days to perform voluntary scouting services. Captain Jack Hays suggested to Flacco that he return with Somervell, and Flacco agreed. It fell to him to lead many of the men, as they had lost confidence in Somervell and refused to recognize him as their commander. They did not trust him to lead them on the long, uncharted, perilous road home. They had more confidence in Flacco.[2]

Jack Hays' scouting revealed that a large Mexican military force was being assembled near Mier, and he urged the

Texans to abandon their plan. Ranger Ben McCulloch added to Hays' information. McCulloch saw Mexican General Antonio Canales Rosillo's troops marching to join Mexican General Ampudia's troops. The Texans were severely outnumbered already, and now massive Mexican reinforcements were on their way. McCulloch told Fisher, "You have had a trap laid.... You will find Ampudia where you expect to find your supplies."[3] In spite of Hays' and McCulloch's warnings, Fisher resolved to cross the Rio Grande. Bigfoot Wallace decided to stay on with Fisher, but he soon regretted it. He later said that in only a few days he wished he had listened to his friends Hays and McCulloch.[4]

Flacco Goes for Horses

When the returning Texans were on the way back toward San Antonio, General Somervell offered Flacco a reward to go to the Nueces River for some horses that had been left there. Flacco went, heading a party of several men, including his

---

Fisher

Born in Virginia, General Fisher was described as "a man of finished education and . . . one of the tallest men in the country. As a conversationalist he was captivating, ever governed by a keen sense of propriety. . . ." (Nance 16)

General Fisher knew the area well. He had fought as a hired soldier in one of the recent Mexican revolts in what is now South Texas and Northern Mexico. He also spoke some Spanish. (Nance 16) He had a distinguished military record, having fought at San Jacinto and having served as Secretary of War. However, he had certain deficits as leader of this expedition. He was such a strong enemy of Sam Houston that he once challenged him to a duel. (Nance 19) Houston did not support a war against Mexico, and Fisher's dislike of Houston might have played a role in his thinking. In addition, the idea of invading Mexico had appealed him for some time. He said he could not "sober down into the country schoolmaster, or the patient drudge; as every other means of subsistence is closed to me . . . my thoughts have latterly reverted towards 'Mexico' . . . this unfortunate and misgoverned Country, presents the fairest field, to a military aspirant, that has . . . offered itself within a Century." (Nance 21)

Indian friend, who was both deaf and mute, and a Tejano named Rivas.

Flacco rounded up fifty horses near the Nueces River. While driving them back, his deaf mute friend fell sick, and the two of them stopped on the Medina River so he could recover. Neither Flacco and his friend, nor the men who had gone with them rejoined Somervell's group, so Somervell and his party finally trudged home without them.

The trip back home was no easier than the one going to the border had been. The returning Texans almost starved. They ate their horses and then fed on roots and herbs. When on January 1, 1843, they reached the San Antonio road, they knew they would make it home alive. They were so happy, they whooped and shouted. One soldier said that to him those shouts sounded like one vast hallelujah.[5]

The Mier Men Organize

While their compatriots were straggling home with Somervell, the Texans under Fisher prepared to cross the Rio Grande into what is now Mexico. General Fisher gave an encouraging talk and tried to make the small force's mission clear. It was to enter Mexico and liberate the San Antonio captives. Fisher warned against pillage. He emphasized that they were engaged in honorable service and that their country would look to them to discharge their duties honorably.[6] The Texans also selected seven captains. Bigfoot Wallace headed the spy company. Thomas Jefferson Green headed a handpicked company which included Asa, Jeffrey, John C. C. Hill, and all the fire eaters. It is easy to understand why 300 men went home. It is less easy to understand why 303 men went on into Mexico. They were without food or warm clothing, and they had very little ammunition. Even so, they decided to challenge the power of a nation. Why did they do it?

Some of them were afraid of being branded as cowards. One of these was George Bernard Erath, twenty-nine, originally from Austria. As a veteran of the Battle of San Jacinto and Captain of the Milam County minute company, he was known as a man of valor and patriotism, so he should not have feared being called a coward. Moreover, he could hardly walk because a cactus needle was painfully lodged deep in his knee. That was reason enough to return home. Yet he later wrote that he lacked the courage to say he wanted to go back.

The importance of being thought courageous and the devastation of being thought a coward can hardly be overestimated. Courage was viewed as essential in a man, and a man's position in the community depended on his reputation. Frontier communities were small and not only a man's social relationships but even his ability to make a living could be endangered if he were shunned as a coward.

Some of the men simply couldn't give up. After marching so many hard-won miles, they couldn't bear to think their efforts were pointless. Some of the volunteers had nothing to return to and thought the trail back to San Antonio would prove harder than the one ahead. Poverty was so desperate and life so hard that they seem to have found some consolation and security from banding together for a cause.

Some of them wanted to make up for the plunder of Laredo. William Fisher said that the soldiers who stayed were "determined to blot out in our own blood, if necessary, the foul stain which has been cast upon us by others" in the sack of Laredo.[7] That he thought fighting Mexicans could make up for the rape of Laredo is an example of his illogical, vainglorious thinking.

Despite all their sufferings, some men were still drunk with the idea of glory in battle. Joseph McCutchan wrote: "There is no sight more grand or sublime than the flash of opposing firearms at the hour of midnight, during one of those times when nature has put on her blackest mantle; and no sound produces such an idea of grandure and engenders such intense excitement as the ringing report of rifles, the hoarse roar of musquetry, the awful thunder of artillery, and encouraging shouts of man, opposed to man, all mingled in dinn and confusion."[8]

CHAPTER 13

Cuidad Mier at Last

December 22, 1842

On December 22, 1842, the men camped on a hill seven miles above the town of Mier. It is about seventy-five miles south of Laredo, and was the largest town on the Rio Grande between Matamoros and Laredo. The Texans also believed it to be the richest. Ironically, on the very same day, Sam Maverick and the other men who had been kidnaped in San Antonio reached their prison—Perote Castle.[1] It is located between Mexico City and Jalapa, hundreds of miles away from the would-be rescuers at Mier. Maverick and his group had walked 2,000 miles.[2]

Fisher decided to march into Mier and demand supplies as the Texans had unsuccessfully done in Laredo and Guerrero. In Laredo, the Texans had been given cakes and hospitality. In Guerrero, they had been given cakes and wet blankets. In Mier they were to find the fight they had come so many miles for.

As the Texans entered the town, Alcalde Francisco Perez, elegant with a silver-headed cane, received the ragged Texans. He invited the officers, Fisher and Green, to the city hall and asked for a list of the supplies the Texan forces needed. The people of Mier, like those of Laredo and Guerrero, were poor farmers who existed on what little they could grow, but the volunteers continued to believe that the Rio Grande Valley was rich and that Mier was one of the richest towns on the Mexican side.

The Texans asked for more supplies than they needed and more than the people of Mier could raise. Texan demands included: 600 pounds of coffee; 1,200 pounds of sugar; 40 sacks of flour; 200 pairs of strong boots; 100 pairs of pantaloons; 100 blankets. They also asked for firearms, powder, lead, and tobacco.

Alcalde Perez diplomatically agreed to all the requests, saying that he had to give supplies to the Mexican army and that he could do no less for the Texans. However, he said that he had no wagons and teams ready to deliver them and that since it was growing dark, he would have them brought to the Texans the next day.

Alcalde Francisco Perez's word was not enough to satisfy General Fisher. He took the alcalde hostage and ordered him to get on his horse and go with the Texans back to camp on the Texas side of the Rio Grande. The elegant alcalde obeyed, but he drooped in his saddle and moaned to himself as the guard escorted him out of Mier.[3]

Some of the Texan soldiers, including John C. C. Hill and the other fire eaters, went down the hill to meet the officers and return to camp with the prisoner. The rough climb up the hill to the camp was no rougher than many other miles the Texans had traveled, but it cost them more. As they struggled toward camp, a shot rang out. Young Jessie Yocum fell to the ground, mortally wounded. One of the Texans' guns had bumped against a mesquite bush and discharged. The bullet hit Yocum in the back. He died instantly.

The Texans buried Yocum in an unmarked grave, covered with rocks to protect it from coyotes. They dared not shoot a volley in his honor because they were too short of ammunition. All the soldiers were deeply moved, and the fire eaters were grieved at the loss of their comrade. Even Alcalde Francisco Perez mourned. "Poor little fellow," he said, "so innocent, so far from home."[4]

Although Perez must have known the ragged Texans had few provisions, he was shocked to find that they had only a few slabs of meat to share with him, and they didn't even have tents. The elegant alcalde was forced to sleep like the Texans, lying on the cold ground with a thin, ragged blanket for cover. Moreover, he had to sleep with his leg between Thomas Jefferson Green's legs to make sure he didn't escape.

Two days passed. The Texans were desperate for food and supplies. On Christmas morning they captured a Mexican sheepherder and found out that General Pedro de Ampudia and General Canales had joined forces and were occupying Mier, just as Hays and McCulloch had warned that they would.

Bigfoot Wallace later told Walter F. McCaleb: "Every time I think about it, I can hardly keep from crying. We were such a bunch of headstrong, foolish men. Many of us were hardly more than boys. We had no common sense. If we had, we would have known that 300 men were no match for 1,500 armed soldiers, supported by cannon. Yet most of us thought we could lick anything."[5]

CHAPTER 14

The Mexican Forces

The Mexican Generals

Both Ewen Cameron and William Fisher were acquainted with the two Mexican generals, Canales and Ampudia. Canales, Fisher, and Cameron had fought for the Federales during the Federalist revolt in Mexico. When the revolt failed, Canales accepted defeat and served the Mexican government he had fought against. Perhaps he was loyal to the larger idea of supporting the Mexican nation, but Cameron and Fisher thought he had sold out, and to them Canales' very name was a synonym for betrayal. Canales and Cameron, former comrades, were now deadly enemies.

General Ampudia had fought against the Federalists in that same conflict. Now the Mexican generals, Canales and Ampudia, former enemies, were on the same side.

General Ampudia had earned the reputation of being both an honorable opponent and a fierce and unfor-

General Ampudia

giving enemy. He once ordered a federalist leader executed, his head cut off and stuck on a pike in front of the man's home in plain sight of his family. This gruesome act was supposed to prevent other revolts. It reveals what a medieval mind General Ampudia had. He is the most contradictory character in this book.

The Mexican Soldiers

Although the Mexican soldiers weren't quite as miserable as the Texans, they were miserable enough. Ampudia's troops had not been paid in four months and had barely been given enough to eat. Like the Texans, they had made an exhausting march through heavy winter rains and across swollen rivers.

Some of the men in Ampudia's force were citizens who were not trained soldiers but were members of local volunteer guards, and others had not joined of their free will, but were criminals who had been forced to serve.

Estimates of the number of Mexican soldiers varied widely, ranging from 90,099 to an inflated 2,340,100. In any event, the 303 Texas volunteers were badly outnumbered.

CHAPTER 15

Before the Battle

The Texans Cross the Rio Grande

In spite of being few against many, the Texans voted to attack. The decision was unanimous, and they set out with perfect confidence, leaving forty men behind to guard their horses and possessions. One of the men left behind was George B. Erath, the young man with a long thorn in his knee. Alcalde Perez asked to be left behind, too. He argued that he had done all he could to help the Texans and that he had a wife and children. The Texans didn't care; they made Perez go with them.

It took until 4:00 P.M. that Christmas Day to get the men across the Rio Grande into Mexico. The river was a broad, deep stream about 1,200 yards wide with high bluffs on the Mexican side.[1]

Ranger Sam Walker Is Captured

Bigfoot's spy company went ahead of the others. At the edge of town, they stumbled into some Mexican cavalrymen and scattered in all directions. Sam Walker and Caleb St. Clair galloped down a side street, but it came to a dead end at a tall fence. They leaped from their horses and clambered up the fence. As St. Clair was climbing, a Mexican cavalryman grabbed his foot to jerk him down. St. Clair's boot came off in the Mexican's hands. He made it across the fence thanks to a loose boot. Sam Walker was not so lucky. A Mexican caught his legs, wrestled him to the ground, and hog-tied him.

Walker was taken to General Ampudia, who asked him how many Texans were in the force, and what their plans were. Ampudia warned Walker that if he reported falsely, he would be executed. Walker replied that his life was in the General's hands, but that Texans didn't lie.

Ampudia again asked how many troops the Texans had.

"Three hundred and three."

"That sounds doubtful to me. It is incredible that you would venture into Mexico with such a handful."

"Well, that's all there are. We had more, but they got tired waiting for a fight and went home."

"With that small number you would not have the audacity to attack."

"You don't know Texans, General. They would pursue and attack you in hell."[2]

Texans Cross the Rio Alamo

By nightfall on Christmas Day 1842, all the scouts except Ranger Sam Walker had made it back to the Texan camp on the steep hill outside Mier and given their reports. Now the 260 volunteers had to cross the Rio Alamo to get into Mier. They could hear horses shaking themselves and rattling gear just across the river. They knew the sound must come from the Mexican cavalry.

General Green led a small detachment to scout out a spot to cross. John C. C. and the other fire eaters went with him. The protesting Alcalde Francisco Perez was forced to go, too, under the guard of an old Irish sea captain, Sailing Master Samuel Lyons. One company stayed behind and opened fire on the enemy across the river to give the impression that they were about to cross there.

General Green placed some of the scouts and boatmen in

a protected spot by the small river embankment. In order to deceive the enemy, they were to open fire on the cavalry stationed on the hill above them. Green fired nine shots from his repeating rifle, then crept downstream to supervise the crossing while the others continued shooting.

The rushing of the river covered the noise of the Texans crossing. General Green's group included Asa and Jeffrey Hill, John C. C., and the other fire eaters. As they pressed toward Mier, they stumbled into a group of mounted Mexican guards.

"*Quién viva?*" the guards cried.

"Let them have it boys!"[3]

About a hundred shots poured into the Mexicans. Not a rifle spoke back. The Texans could hear a Mexican colonel a few hundred yards away shouting for the cavalry to charge, but the horsemen refused. They retreated into Mier.

Joseph Berry Falls

In the meantime, Captain Charles Keller Reese and Joseph Berry went downstream to fire at a guard. As they scrambled over rocks on their way back, Berry fell into a ravine and broke his leg. Reese fetched the doctor, John J. Sinnickson, and seven other soldiers. They tied a rope around Berry and managed to pull him up and carry him to a nearby, abandoned adobe hut.

The Alcalde Escapes

A different group of Texans followed Green down the bluff in single file. Sammy Lyons and his captive, Alcalde Perez, were with them. They crossed the Rio Alamo at a place where the river made enough noise to cover the sound of their movements, but some Mexican cavalry spotted them and opened fire.

The Texans shot back. Sammy Lyons, excited by at last being in combat, opened fire with his double barreled Joe

Manton gun. Alcalde Perez seized the moment and slipped away in the darkness.⁴

"Where's the alcalde?" shouted General Green.

"Shure, sor, an' he's gone adhr-rift!" the old Irish sea dog admitted.⁵ He had lost the Texans' bargaining chip, but a laugh ran down the line of soldiers when they heard him.

Fisher Fails to Act

Green crept forward into Mier to find the position of the Mexican forces. General Fisher and the Texans waited outside Mier under cover of darkness. Mexican soldiers fired from the rooftops. A few Texans returned their fire, betraying their position. Quickly, Captain Claudius Buster "cooly ordered his men to kneel, and well it was that he gave this order; for, although the night was dark, the Mexican balls were so well directed that they fell like hail against a wall immediately in the rear of Buster's company."⁶ For a few minutes the Texans waited for Fisher to command them, but he gave no orders. Captain Buster took charge and told his men to return fire. During the shooting, a musket ball flew so near Bigfoot that he felt the wind of its passing. It struck and killed his comrade, John Jones of Houston.⁷

CHAPTER 16

The Battle at Cuidad Mier

John Taney livened up the entry into Mier by whistling like a fife.[1] The town was dark; the streets were deserted except for Ampudia's men, who were ready and waiting. The Mexican artillery fired from the street; the infantry fired from rooftops.

Texan soldiers took cover in a house at the corner of a street leading to the plaza. The houses were built with their outer walls touching. The Texans knocked holes in the walls, making a passage through the houses. They wanted to take out the Mexican's cannon that was in the middle of the square. The two Texan companies managed to get into the houses on opposite sides of the street. Well hidden and well sheltered, the Texans could then shoot into the plaza from two sides.

Some Mexican families had leaped up from the supper table and rushed out, leaving warm food behind. Half-starved Texans snatched it.

All of the houses were empty except one in which a baby had been left behind. Ignoring the gunfire, Bigfoot carried the baby out, shouted for the Mexicans to come and get the child, and gently dropped it over the wall.[2]

In one of the rooms, the men found a bottle of *aguardiente* and began drinking it like water. One of the officers drank so much, he fell on the floor and was wounded by a bullet that came through a crack.³ Bigfoot, who was never a drinker, poured out the rest of the firewater.

Serious fighting began before sunrise. The Mexicans fired at the houses, but the grapeshot and even the cannon balls did not completely go through the thick adobe walls. Instead, most of the shots bounced back into the street along with chunks of adobe and brick.

Joseph Berry Is Killed

As the fighting raged, the men on the other side of the Rio Alamo river watched from the distance. They had struggled to get Joseph Berry, with his broken leg, up the ravine, onto high ground, and into the hut. It had taken their united strength to hold him down as he flailed in anguish while Dr. Sinnickson set his leg. Now, however, they felt useless and condemned to the sidelines, watching from the distance as the battle raged in Mier.

Then they saw sixty Mexican cavalrymen coming up from the ford. The Mexicans galloped by the hut, not suspecting that the Texans were in it. The volunteers could have simply laid low, but they foolishly fired. Each brought down a victim and the other Mexicans scattered, then regrouped and trained a cannon on the Texans in the hut. They fired and missed, but the Texans thought that the next shot would crumble the hut to dust. They could not survive repeated cannon fire. They decided that if they ran, the Mexican force would follow them. Then the hut would not be fired on and Joseph Berry might have a chance in spite of his broken leg.⁴ Also, they might be able to join their friends in battle. So the Texans, except for wounded Joseph Berry, his brother Bate, and Dr. Sinnickson, dashed for the river. But the Mexican soldiers did go into the hut. They bayonetted Joseph Berry in his bed in spite of his brother's pleas.⁵ The other men fled for their lives. The cavalry ran them down. They killed three and took three captive, including Dr. Sinnickson. Only Bate Berry escaped. He reached the Texan stronghold in Mier safely.

The Fire Eaters Defeat the Cannon

General Green stationed John C. C. Hill and the other fire eaters about fifty yards from the cannon in a protected spot that would let them use their sharp-shooting skills.

"Boys, that battery of theirs makes too much noise. You must stop it! It might kill somebody by accident!" Green joked. "Every time you see a man try to load that cannon, take good aim and hit him in the head. Don't fire at the same time, keep cool, and don't quit until you get your orders."[6]

Immediately, John C. C. looked down the sight of his rifle and pulled the trigger. He caught an artilleryman in the temple.

The fire eaters aimed, fired, and reloaded each in turn. One by one, they picked off the men firing the cannon. John C. C. learned that his brother Jeffrey had been wounded. It was hard not to worry about that, but he concentrated on his task.

The cannon had been manned at dawn. By nine o'clock that morning, fifty-five gunners were dead and five were disabled.[7] The young fire eaters had made it certain death to go near the cannon, so it was left unused and silent. Finally the Mexicans lassoed it and pulled it back to a sheltered position. Then the fire eaters turned to other targets.

The Battle Rages

On the rooftops, Mexican shooters had the protection of a three-foot high wall, but they had to peer over it to fire. Texan sharp shooters picked them off. A "sickening stream of human blood flowed from the gutters and, curdling in the December cold, formed great hideous heaps, sometimes fully a foot in height!"[8]

General Ampudia withdrew the infantry from the rooftops, lined them up in the plaza, and made a direct assault on the Texans. About fifty Texans left the protection and the tactical advantage of the houses and lined up in the conventional battle style of the day to meet the assault. Instead of

sticking to the guerilla style of warfare they were so good at, they actually followed General Ampudia's lead into a different style of fighting.

Both sides fired. In spite of the foolish decision to line up, face the enemy, and exchange shots, the Texans came out ahead. Their sharpshooting skills and their superior weapons served them well. When the smoke cleared, they saw that many Mexicans lay dead. Only two Texans were lost. However, several Texans were injured. Fisher's right thumb was shattered by a musket ball.

Bigfoot Wallace, eager in battle, all alone pursued a group of retreating Mexicans. Suddenly they turned on him, and he realized he was in trouble. "I was determined . . . to retreat at all hazards, and turned and dashed through their line. One fellow, as I passed, made a lunge at me with his bayonet, slightly wounding me in the left arm, but I made good my escape and rejoined my comrades, who had given me up."[9]

Joseph D. McCutchan, nineteen, gave a dramatic account of the battle. He said that William Ryon was "down but up again as if by magic, while his eye was still fierce and nerved for the contest." Ewen Cameron and his Western boys were as "immovable as the rock of ages." Cameron carried a "death dealing Yager." Texan rifles "belched forth death to the foe."[10]

Some of the men never lost their romantic view. One was Henry Weeks. He fought heroically and was shot twice. He suffered "wounds that seemingly would have disabled ordinary men at each of the two shots." He fought on. When he was hit a third time, friends carried him to a house. He begged them to let him "remain in the street to witness the glory of the arms of Texas."[11]

Twice more Ampudia ordered an assault; twice more Mexicans fell in heaps while the Texans suffered few losses. The unreliable Mexican flintlock guns probably misfired because of the light rain; the Texans' percussion-cap rifles were less affected by weather.

The Texans were carrying the day. They were incredibly daring; they had amazing endurance; and they were brilliant marksmen. According to Methodist minister Whitfield Chalk, "The way the Mexicans fell was a caution," and another participant wrote, "The way our riflemen picked them off was a sin to Davy Crockett."[12]

But the Texans were outnumbered and low on ammunition. As at Hondo, they lacked military discipline. Every soldier was his own general. The Texan force fell into confusion. General Thomas Jefferson Green knew the generals must regain control. He jumped onto a table and tried to shout above the noise, but everyone else was shouting orders, too.

General Ampudia sent 100 militiamen to attack from the rear. Captain Ewen Cameron, in his tattered tartan plaid, with a bowie knife in his belt, found the Mexicans massing behind a stone wall. When his ammunition ran out, he shouted, "Boys, to your stones!"[13] Cameron's "Men-Slayers,"[14] fifty strong, smashed heads and confounded the enemy. The Mexicans were driven back by the barrage of rocks, but three of Cameron's men lay dead and seven were wounded. One fifth of his men were unable to fight. "Keep your heads down," he yelled. "I'll run for aid."[15]

Ampudia Uses Wile; Texans Lose Will

General Ampudia made no more efforts to dislodge the Texans. The streets were quiet and deserted. Then a lone man walked toward them carrying a white flag. A cheer went up; the Texans thought the victory was theirs. But the flag was not a flag of surrender. It was carried by the reluctant Dr. Sinnickson, who was forced to present the Mexican demand. The Texans were to be granted a one hour cease fire. At the end of that time, if the Texans did not yield, fighting would resume. No quarter would be given—the Mexicans would take no prisoners. All would be killed, as they were at the Alamo, but if the Texans surrendered, they would be treated as prisoners of war and would not be marched to Mexico City. Instead, they would be kept in the Rio Grande Valley. However, all the promises depended on Santa Anna's approval. The Mexicans also declared that peace negotiations were beginning and the Texans would therefore not be captive for long.[16]

General Fisher walked up the square, talked to General Ampudia, and turned down the Mexican offer. Ampudia, speaking politely, said that hostilities would "resume in ten minutes."[17]

CHAPTER 17

Surrender

Fisher's wounded thumb proved to be a fateful injury. He was weak from loss of blood and from hunger. As he walked back toward his men, several of them passed him on their way to the plaza, perhaps to surrender. He ordered them to stop, but they ignored him. He implored them to stop. They ignored him. Because of this incident and because of the general disorder, Fisher decided he had lost control of the troops. He felt that the Texans' slender chance of winning was now completely gone, so he went back to General Ampudia and said he had changed his mind.

Fisher later said that he felt obligated to preserve the lives of his men and that he had refused to listen to "the clamor of a few harebrained men and silly boys" who still wanted to fight their way out of Mier.[1] However, Fisher's decision was viewed by some as bad judgment.

General Green believed that Fisher's wound had weakened his spirit and had caused him to yield. Bigfoot Wallace said he never understood why they stopped fighting and surrendered when they were winning. James Glasscock and Israel Canfield both reported that they learned from some of the Mexican officers that if General Fisher hadn't given in, the Mexicans would have left Mier because they were losing too many men to continue.[2]

It was true that the Texans were on foot, far from home, without ammunition, and that Ampudia had closed all the routes out of town. Also, disorder and lack of discipline were serious problems, as they always were with the Texans. However, the Mexicans had suffered immense casualties, and the Texans might have been able to seize Mexican supplies. Some felt that their chance of doing so was as great as their chance of surviving after surrender.

Indeed, many of them would have fought with the butts of their guns rather than give in, and they cursed the men who gave up. All the fire eaters were ready to fight to the end. General Green later said, "Had our men at Mier been boys, I do not entertain a doubt that I should have been spared the pain of recording their captivity, sufferings, and deaths."[3]

But the battle was over. General Fisher had surrendered

The Texans Argue

The Texan volunteer force was run on democratic principles, and General Fisher's decision did not necessarily mean that the men would follow him, but the possibility of surrender was now up for serious consideration. Fisher had to persuade the volunteers that this was the best course of action. He explained the situation to the men and they discussed it.

General Ampudia had promised that the captives would be treated "with consideration which is in accordance — with the magnanimous Mexican nation."[4] Many of the men believed they were taken as prisoners of war, but that would have meant that Santa Anna's government acknowledged Texas as an independent country, and it refused to do this. To the Mexican government, Texas was a part of Mexico that was in revolt, and the men who fought at Mier were rebels and criminals.

Fisher understood the terms of the surrender. It basically gave the Texans their lives and nothing else. He told the men, "I have known General Pedro de Ampudia for years. I know him to be an honorable man and will vouch that he will carry out his promises."[5]

General Fisher was accurate in his assessment of General Ampudia's character, but power lay with Santa Anna. Fisher did not make it clear to the men that the terms of surrender gave the Texans only their lives and gave no details about how they would be treated. Ampudia had made no specific promises.

Even without being told the truth that there were no guarantees as to their treatment, many of the Texans disagreed with Fisher. They remembered how other Mexican commanders had betrayed their vows. Bigfoot's brother and cousin who had surrendered at Goliad were betrayed and massacred. Bigfoot felt sure General Ampudia's promises were a trick.

"If we give in, they'll kill us sure,"[6] Bigfoot warned. "Beware of the Mexicans when they press you to hot coffee and 'tortillas.' Put fresh caps on your revolver, and see that your 'shooting-irons' are all in order, for you will probably need them before long. He will feed you on his best, 'señor'

Chalk and St. Clair Sneak Out

While the Texans debated, Whitfield Chalk and Caleb St. Clair realized that there was going to be a surrender whether they agreed or not. They slipped away from the group, and hid in an oven in the courtyard of one of the houses. There they waited for an opportunity to escape.

Chalk and St. Clair sneaked out of town that night—the fateful December 26, 1842. St. Clair, who had his boot pulled off as he was climbing a fence, still had only one boot, and his ankle was badly sprained. Slowed by that injury, the two men traveled all night through thick scrub brush and cactus. They reached the Rio Grande at dawn. Some of the forty men who had been left at the Texan camp on the Texas side of the Rio Grande heard them call and crossed over and got them. Chalk and St. Clair told them the sad news of the Texan surrender. Then, bit by bit, the men broke camp, leaving for home in small groups to avoid attracting attention. They had a long way to go, and game was scarce except for wild horse. It would be a hard road home.

George Bernard Erath and William Oldham traveled with Chalk and St. Clair. At Goliad, they met Rangers Ben and Henry McCulloch. Chalk and St. Clair made it home January 19, 1843. (Wade 116) Along with Erath, they carried the first news of the surrender at Mier to La Grange.

you, and *'muchas gracias'* you, and bow to you like a French dancing-master, and wind it all up by slipping a knife under your left shoulder-blade![7]

Like Bigfoot, Ewen Cameron and his men were dead set against surrender. Cameron, in his Scottish accent said, "By God, General, me and the whole of my company will go it!"[8] General Thomas Jefferson Green didn't want to surrender either. He wanted the Texans to fight their way out of town. Captain Cameron shouted that if as many as one hundred men would stand by him, he would lead them out even if he had to cut their way through the enemy line.[9]

But the other Texans wanted to surrender. At last, General Green gave in, but he said, "We will all be sacrificed ... Now we will see who can stand shooting best."[10] Ewen Cameron and his men still stood firm.

John C. C. and Asa Hill joined Ewen Cameron and the men who opposed surrender. More than forty Texans stood by the valiant Scot. "Keep on fighting, Captain. We'll follow you to hell!"

Finally Cameron said, "Boys, it is no use to continue the fight any longer. They are all gone but us, and we will have to knock under."[11]

Texans Yield Their Arms

"The first to surrender were three men who filed out while 'yet in tears' to cast down their arms. Every few minutes a few weary, battle-worn Texans, with faces begrimed and often streaked with tears ... entered the plaza to stack their arms at the feet of a Mexican officer."[12]

Sadly, Cameron led his men into the patio. They laid down their rifles, revolvers, knives, powder horns, and their catskin and tiger-tailed pouches. Bigfoot Wallace was one of the last. Later he said, "When we were stripped of our arms ... I could have cried if I hadn't been so mad."[13]

John C. C. Hill felt even worse than Bigfoot. He had promised to take care of his father and Jeffrey, and he had vowed that Santa Anna's soldiers would never shoot James Monroe Hill's treasured gun.

All eyes, Mexican and Texan, were on thirteen year old John C. C. as he walked forward — the youngest, the smallest, and the last to surrender.

Suddenly John C. C. whirled his gun in the air, caught it by the barrel and smashed it on the pavement stones. The gun stock splintered into fragments, and John C. C. dropped the ruined gun.

Amid shouts from the Mexicans, John C. C. took his place by his father. He couldn't understand what the people were shouting in Spanish. He heard hands clapping, but he did not realize that the Mexicans were applauding his valor, or that General Ampudia was looking down on the square and was charmed by his defiance.

CHAPTER 18
John C. C. and General Ampudia

Shortly afterward, a Mexican officer signaled John C. C. to come with him. John C. C. fell in behind the officer, and an armed soldier followed. The eyes of the captive Texans followed the small form. As John C. C. turned the corner and passed from their sight, Asa Hill gave a groan.[1]

John C. C. followed the officer through the wrought iron gateway of Garcia Mansion. They passed between sentinels and up stone steps into a hallway. John C. C. was led into a long drawing room to face General Ampudia. Dark and bearded, the General was seated in an armchair. His own son, Don Miguel, had been mortally wounded in the battle that day.

General Ampudia was a commanding figure. He wore a belt and sword, and his uniform was decorated with gold braid. Medals adorned his chest. Around him were staff officers and orderlies, brilliant in their dress uniforms.

John C. C. stood before the General. He was small for his age and wore moccasins and rags, but he looked like a soldier. His face was streaked with grime. He held his battered felt hat in one hand.

"*Hijito*, do not be afraid. I will not harm you." General Ampudia extended his arm as he spoke.

John C. C. stepped forward into the shelter of the protecting arm. He heaved a sigh of relief. In this moment, he was not a young soldier facing the enemy; he was a boy finding comfort in the embrace of a kind adult—an adult whose son he might have shot.

"You are very young to be a soldier. Have Texans so few men that they must send their little ones to battle?" General Ampudia asked.

An officer interpreted.

"I am no *little one*. I am thirteen years old."

"A thousand apologies, señor," said the courtly General. "I did not know. It is a manly age. What is your name?"

"John Christopher Columbus Hill."

"Ah, Juan Cristobal Colon Gil. A good Spanish name. And what did you expect to discover in Mexico?"

"I came to fight Mexicans."

"Have you no father?"

"Why yes, he is out there with my brother, Jeffrey."

"How is it when you had a father and brother to send to war that you did not stay with your mother?"

"My brother, James Monroe, is with my mother and sisters. He fought at San Jacinto. It was my turn to go."

"Why did you break your rifle, Juan?"

Then John C. C. told General Ampudia the story of being given the rifle and how his parents had decided that it was God's will that he should go to help his father and brother.

"Tell me, Juan, are you one of those boys who did such deadly work to my Captain Castro's battery?"

"Yes, sir. General Green put the boys and me to pick off the men at the cannon. He told us to take good aim and not miss or the cannon would tear the wall down and kill a whole lot of us. So we were very careful."

"I am sure of that, my son. You and your companions make fine soldiers because you obey orders."

General Ampudia asked the names of the other fire eaters. He wrote them down carefully and gave them to a soldier. The interview was over.

"Follow this officer. He will see that you have food and rest."

John C. C. hesitated. Then he spoke. "But my father and brother . . . They'll think I am going to be shot!"

"Oh, no, *hombrecito*. They will be told. You will see them tomorrow."

"But Jeffrey is wounded."

"I will ask that my surgeon watch over him."

General Ampudia's kindness reassured John C. C. He left the general's presence with some of the burdens lifted from his heart. When he got to his room and found the other fire eaters there, he was almost happy.

General Ampudia's Grief

John C. C. Hill, the captured young Texan, had more reason to be happy than General Ampudia, the victorious Mexican general. John C. C. could not know that the man who treated him so kindly, was himself in terrible grief, but General Fisher and General Green soon knew.

When they were taken to Ampudia's headquarters to receive the "Articles of Capitulation," General Green took off his sword belt and gave it to General Ampudia. "I am General Green. I have opposed the surrender in vain. I am prepared for prison or to be shot and am perfectly indifferent to the choice."

General Ampudia bowed. "I appreciate the feelings of the brave, but yours is the fate of war. My house and friendship are yours. I hope you will consider yourself my guest."[2]

General Ampudia's son, Don Miguel, was in the same room on a pallet on the floor writhing in his death agony. The young man, only twenty-six years old, was a graduate of Chapultepec Military Academy. He had attained the rank of colonel and was adjutant-general of the Mexican forces.

General Ampudia dearly loved his handsome and intelligent son, but he had to carry on with his duties even as his son lay dying. General Ampudia kept his dignified bearing, but there were tears in his eyes when he said, "There is my son, the hope of the army, the pride of the service. He has a death-shot through the kidneys and must soon die."

General Green expressed his and General Fisher's sympathy in the formal language considered proper in that day. "I hope you will accept my sympathy in this your great sorrow, but this is the fate of war. The dead in all ranks share our sympathy."[3]

CHAPTER 19

After the Battle

Burying the Dead

Church bells tolled all day for the men killed in battle. Bigfoot Wallace estimated that more than 800[1] Mexican soldiers were slain. Soldiers used ropes to lower their dead comrades from rooftops where they had fallen. All the Mexican dead were taken to the square. From the place where the Texans surrendered, he saw four rows of Mexican bodies close together. The rows stretched across the plaza. Priests were among them. Later ox carts were loaded with the bodies. They were taken to a ditch outside of town to be buried in a common grave.

"While this was being done, the bodies of the slain Texans, stripped of their clothing, were being dragged through the streets by the cavalry, followed by crowds of yelling Mexicans of all sizes and ages."[2]

The Kindness of Women

Townspeople returned to their homes. Both citizens and soldiers cleaned the town. In spite of having lost so many of their own men, Mexican women took pity on the Texan prisoners and fed them, passing them tortillas, red peppers, and *cabrito* through the gratings of the windows. This was the first of many kind gestures Mexican women extended to the captive Texans.

Bigfoot Wallace told of looking hungrily out of a grating, when a little Mexican maiden came tripping along and saw his woebegone face. She brought him tortillas, red peppers and "a considerable chunk of roast kid meat." He made her a low bow. She went away laughing, and he lost sight of his "pumpkin-colored angel forever."[3]

The Wounded

Twenty-three Texans were seriously wounded in the battle. John Day Morgan "carried his friend and neighbor, James Barber, into the hospital, the poor fellow being wounded in the breast." Barber knew he didn't have long to live. He asked Morgan to tell his family, "I die for Texas !"[4]

Together General Ampudia and General Green visited the wounded Texans who were on pallets in the church. Some of them had head wounds that bled onto the floor with clots as big as marbles. The Texans joked in the face of disaster.

Green asked them, "How are you for rations?"

"Oh, we have plenty of brains," the Texans answered.[5]

They made jokes about John C. C. Hill's clothes, too, when he brought breakfast to his father and Jeff. General Ampudia had given "Don Juan" a fine suit. The white linen shirt, red sash, and short black jacket were hardly what a Texan expected to wear. John C. C. later said he thought he must look like a traitor — he didn't even carry the food himself, but was followed by a servant with a tray.

Jeffrey lay on a pallet wounded and without trousers. Mexican soldiers had stripped him. Asa, beside him, looked exhausted and worried, but both he and Jeff made light of their situation.

Dr. Sinnickson also joked. "Well, Don Juan, you've landed on your feet! Why you young scoundrel, you have a gold mine in that good looking face!"

John C. C., embarrassed, answered, "I wish I was ugly as . . ."

"As I am." Dr. Sinnickson finished John C. C.'s sentence

for him. "Don't be a fool. The Mexicans are probably afraid of you, young tiger. Go back and scare them into giving you some good things for poor lantern-jawed, knock-kneed, crooked nosed, red-headed sinners like me and Jeff."

All the Texans' good humor and lack of envy helped John C. C., but he was in a confusing situation. Yesterday the Mexicans were his enemies. Only a few hours ago he had been killing them. Now he was living among them, dressed like them, and accepting their charity.

Asa's Advice

Asa understood that John C. C. was now having a war inside himself. Though not a man given to much speech, Asa talked seriously with his son.

"I believe General Ampudia is an honorable gentlemen, and we know he is a kind one. You fought well, but you were conquered. You expected death, but you are given kindness. Accept it in the spirit in which it is given."

But it seemed wrong to John C. C. that he should be dressed in fine clothes, eating good food, and sleeping in a soft bed when his father, his brother, and his friends were in terrible circumstances. "I promised Mother to take care of you!" John C. C. protested.

"You can help us more where you are than if you were shut up with us," Asa told him.

John C. C. hadn't thought of that.

Jeffrey, concealing the pain of his wound, chimed in. "You are spunky, but you ain't got your growth. Eat all you can. We don't want to take any skinny boy back to Mother."

Asa put a coin in John C. C.'s hand. "See if you can get Jeff some wine, son!"

John C. C. handed it back. "See, Father, what the General has put in my pocket." He pulled out a handful of coins.

"Get out of here before I rob you!" Dr. Sinnickson joked.

Jeffrey added, "And see if you can't find me some pants like yours, with gold in the pockets."

Waiting Again

The Texans were used to waiting, but the five days they were imprisoned at Mier were long days. They didn't know what would happen to them. Some of them thought they would be freed and allowed to go home. Others thought they would be shot.

The captive Texans saw themselves of rural knights on a glorious crusade, but Mexico saw them as traitors out for plunder. General Ampudia would have been within his authority to execute the Texans as common criminals. In kindness, he chose instead to consider them prisoners of war.

General Fisher and General Green were treated as if they were educated gentlemen with serious military credentials. They were housed and fed like General Ampudia himself.

The soldiers had it harder, but so did the Mexican soldiers, and General Ampudia was merciful to the men like John Day Morgan who had been on the Santa Fe expedition. They had promised never to take up arms against Mexico again on pain of death, but Ampudia treated them just like the other prisoners.

All the fire eaters were given special consideration because of their youth. They were clothed, well fed, and kindly treated.

Yet this civilized and gracious General Ampudia was the same man who had ordered a Mexican federalist leader executed, then ordered his head chopped off and stuck on a pike in front of his house.

CHAPTER 20

Flacco Is Murdered

James O. Rice, who had bribed his way out of Mier, discovered the bodies of Flacco and his deaf-mute friend about 20 miles west of San Antonio. They had been murdered.

News of the murder spread, and rumors spread with it. Many people believed that Flacco was betrayed by his Texan companions.

Some people said that Flacco and his deaf mute friend were murdered by the Tejanos who had gone with them to get horses for Somervell. These people said that the Tejanos drove the horses into Eastern Texas and Louisiana and sold them.[1]

According to other accounts of the murder, two white men were missing from Somervell's group the morning after Flacco and his sick friend were left behind. In this version, the two white men were seen in Seguin with Flacco's horses a few days later.

Young Flacco had been the apple of his father's eye and an idolized leader in the tribe. When his father, Old Chief Flacco, learned that the expedition had returned and young Flacco was not with them, he went to Noah Smithwick for help.

Smithwick had a gun shop in Webber's Prairie. Since he spoke Spanish and the Indians knew more Spanish than English, friendly Indians used to gather in his shop. He frequently interpreted for them. He was well acquainted with young Flacco and with his family. Old Flacco and his wife had often visited the Smithwicks at their home. They had brought the Smithwicks gifts of game and brought little beaded moccasins for their small son.

Smithwick was used to seeing Indians accept sorrow without showing emotion, but tears ran down Old Flacco's face and sobs shook his frame. Smithwick later wrote, "I felt how useless words were in such a crisis. I could only express my sympathy by the tears that welled up in my own eyes."[2]

At Old Chief Flacco's request, Smithwick wrote President Houston and General Burleson asking them to investigate.

Several days later, Old Flacco and his wife came to see the Smithwicks. Flacco's parents were in such grief that they had not eaten for several days and were so starved that they

---

Escape and Homecoming

A wealthy Texan visiting Mexico, Henry Lawrence Kinney, pretended to be a U.S. citizen and so was allowed to visit the wounded at Mier. He gave James Rice $500 for food and clothing, but Rice used the money to bribe the guard. On December 26, the guard escorted Rice and seven others outside Mier. He gave them food and three guns, set them on their way, and told them that he would lead the pursuit in the wrong direction along the Palo Blanco Road.

The Texans got lost, wandered in the chaparral, and found themselves at the Palo Blanco Road. The Mexican cavalry was coming. The Texans had to get away. They had to cross the road, but that would leave a trail. Irish William Rupley had the solution. In a broad accent, he said, "By the Holy Saint Patrick can't we just walk across the road backwards, and make the devils think we are going the other way?" (Nance 209)

They did. Then they limped and hobbled the long way to Victoria. They hunted on the way but only killed two mule-rabbits and two buzzards.

Robert Harper Beale, who had been shot through the lung in the battle, made it home by mid-March looking "more like a ghost than a man." (Nance 210) A merchant in the community, Thompson McMahan, was so overjoyed to see Beale alive, he grabbed him in a bear hug. The hug broke Beale's wound open, and he almost bled to death because of the enthusiastic welcome. (The group consisted of James O. Rice, Robert H. Beale, George B. Pilant, Henry D. Weeks, William Rupley, Nathaniel R. Mallon, John Bidler, and Lewis Hays. [Nance 209])

looked like mummies. Mrs. Smithwick prepared dinner and persuaded them to eat a little.

Later when Houston's answer arrived, it said that young Flacco and his friend had been murdered by Mexican bandits. There was also a letter from Señor Antonio Navarro, a prominent San Antonio merchant and a trusted friend of the Lipans, confirming the sad story. Smithwick interpreted the letters from Houston and Navarro as delicately as he could.[3]

Smithwick himself felt sure the two white men had murdered Flacco and stolen the horses, but he did not dare tell the old chief that. He believed that if the Lipans had known how young Flacco really died, they would have fought to the death against the whites, and "the crime of one miserable wretch would have caused the death of hundreds of innocent people."[4]

Shortly after that, the tribe left the area, going toward the Rio Grande. There were only about sixty warriors in the tribe.

The betrayal and murder of Flacco is one of the saddest stories in Texas history.

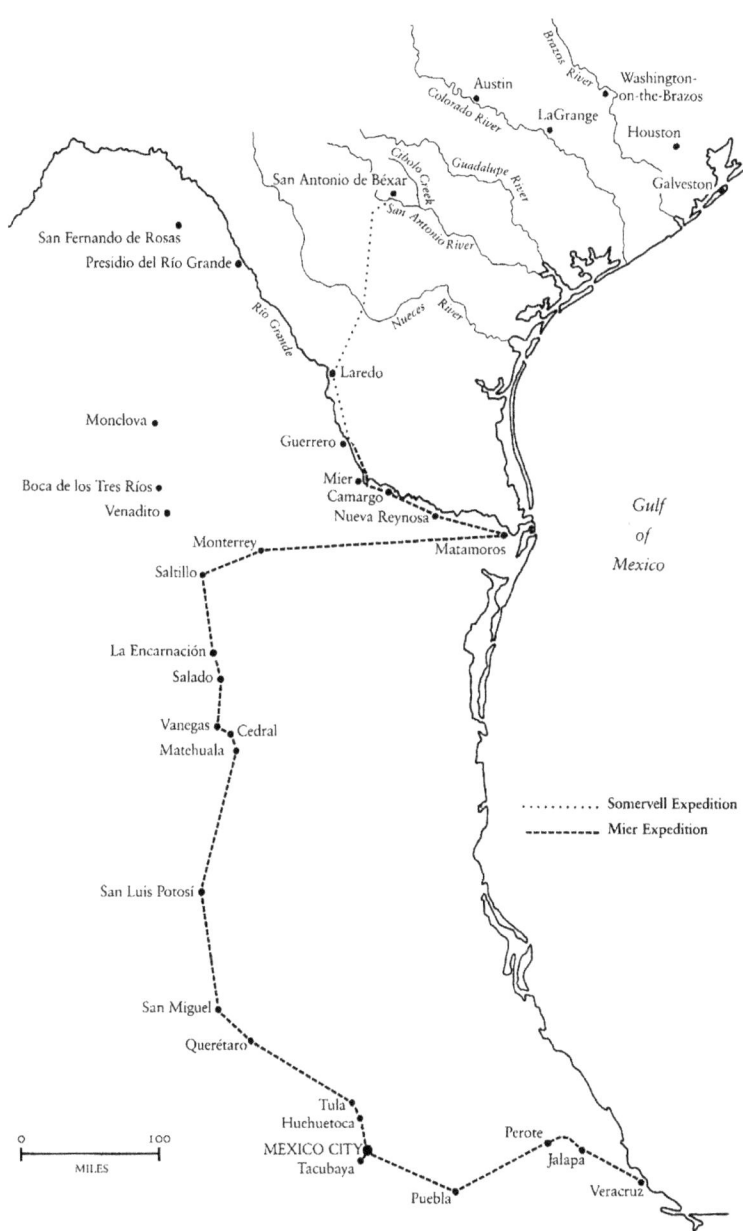

The Somervell and Mier Expeditions

CHAPTER 21

The Captive Mier Men on the Road

On December 31, 1842, after a five-day wait, Ampudia was ready to return to his home in Matamoros. The 217 captives were marched out of Mier in double file, guarded by 800 Mexican infantry and cavalry, "an ample guard for the half-starved, unarmed" Texans whose combined possessions "could easily have been packed in a lady's bonnet box."[1] The number of guards equaled the number of Mexican soldiers the Texans had killed.

A military band played. General Ampudia and John C. C. Hill headed the procession, followed by a cannon, General Ampudia's staff, General Fisher, and General Green. Three fire eaters, Billy Reese, Harvey Sellers, and Orlando Phelps, also followed, and a second cannon brought up the rear.[2]

Asa Hill was one of the few Texans who rode a horse. John C. C. had asked General Ampudia to see that his father didn't have to walk. Dr. Sinnickson and interpreter John Brennan were left behind with the twenty-one surviving wounded, including Jeffrey Barksdale Hill.

They marched beside the Rio Grande along a high limestone ridge. Some had on high heeled boots; some had no shoes at all, and they were continually prodded by bayonets and ox goads.[3] Bigfoot commented:

I have seen men when broken down and "beat out" by a hard day's march, wake up to new life and energy on the receipt of some welcome news, and, under like circumstance, I have seen renewed vigor instilled into them by the spirited strains of a fine band of music; but nothing is so effective in this way as one or two inches of cold steel in the body. I know this is so, for I speak from sad personal experience . . .[4]

The men were not allowed to stop for water and suffered terribly from thirst. At sunset, they reached a ranch outside the small town of Camargo on the San Juan River. A bleak norther blew in. It seemed to echo the men's misery and to predict more misery to come. There was no building at the ranch for the Texan soldiers to stay in. They were fastened in a corral where only the fence gave slight protection from the cold wind.

The Texans, in their rambunctious way, took the hardship in stride. They dropped down on their hands and knees and pawed the ground. Some of them bleated like hungry calves; others bellowed like bulls. Finally the puzzled Mexicans realized that the Texans were making fun of their situation, and they laughed at their strange captives' joke. The fun over, the Texans built some small campfires, and when the fires burned low, they scraped away the coals and lay down in the warm ashes, but the biting wind cut away the possibility of sleep.

The next day, January 1, 1843, they were taken into the town itself. Cheering crowds lined the streets of Camargo. The entire population of 600 people had turned out to welcome the victorious Mexican troops. Bells rang, but they were not exactly melodious. Indeed, they clattered so loudly it seemed as if they were going to break loose and fling themselves into the air.[5] Paper banners announced the Mexican victory at Mier and praised General Ampudia. People placed poles from rooftop to rooftop across the narrow streets and hung all kinds of bright colored fabric on them. Scarves, rebozos, ladies pink undergarments, and men's silver-buttoned trousers were the banners that announced the captives arrival. The Texans were marched around the square three times as the bells of the church rang out. That night the soldiers had shelter, at least; they were confined in a brick building.

John C.C., the other fire eaters, and the commanding officers fared much better. They were taken to the home of a kind gentleman, Don Trinidad. Their windows looked out onto a patio shaded by orange and lemon trees — a reflection of grace and gentility. The stark difference in John C. C.'s circumstances and those of his father and brother can only have been painful and puzzling to him.

Odd Doings at Nueva Reynosa

Two days later, when the Texans reached Nueva Reynosa, they experienced a particularly remarkable celebration. As they went up a steep hill, a group of Carrizo Indians, dressed only in breech-clouts and decorated with war paint, suddenly appeared in their path. They whooped and fired blank charges into the Texans' faces. Then the Indians reloaded and repeated the maneuver. Some of the startled Texans were angry; some were amused.

To the Texans further surprise, an old man, tiny as a twelve year old, appeared leading about twenty little boys in a dance. They had different colored ribbons and handkerchiefs attached to their clothes and they wore four-sided, mirrored towers on their heads. Each carried a gourd rattle decorated with blue and yellow paper. Several fiddlers provided music.

The boys and their old leader hopped on one foot, shook the other foot, and shook the gourds, dancing in perfect time with the fiddles. They danced the Texans into town where they entered through a triumphal arch made of reeds and decorated with colored cloth. Banners inscribed: "gloria," "inmortalidad," and "honor"[6] waved in the breeze. Ladies cheered from housetops; men shouted; Indians yelled, church bells clattered, and people danced in the street.

The Texans were paraded through town and three times around the central square. The people of Reynosa hooted, spit, threw stones, and tossed rotten eggs. At last, the Texans were marched to their quarters in an unfinished brick building where they lay down for the night on a cold stone floor to be tormented by fleas and lice.

On To Matamoros

On January 6, 1843, the prisoners were again marched to the Reynosa plaza. They were made to stand at attention for two hours. Mass was said, followed by the shooting of fireworks and the firing of cannon.

Then they began their march to Matamoros, all except a man named Samuel McDade, who was ill. The Texans were forced to leave him behind, lying on a piece of rawhide, where he soon died.[7] The other Texans arrived in Matamoros on January 9. Again, they entered to the sound of drums, fifes, and pealing horns from the military band.[8]

General Ampudia was given a lavish reception at his home. John C. C. stayed with him and met the friends and dignitaries who visited. Once a Mexican colonel put his hand on John C. C.'s head and said, "You are too small; they would run over you in battle."

John C. C. remembered shooting the Mexicans at the cannon. He answered, "As small as I am, I made twelve of your countrymen bow low to me the other day."[9]

As the Texans marched into each of the towns, their guards were questioned by friends and relatives who did not see their loved ones among the Mexican soldiers. The frantic relatives received an answer the Texans did not need Spanish to understand. It was "a sudden stroke upon the forehead with the end of the forefinger and a significant shrug of the shoulders, which invariably produced a shriek of woe."[10]

Though the Texans met ridicule and hostility, they met other attitudes, as well. Many people were simply curious to see the wild Texans, whom they seemed to regard as less than human. Others felt sorry for them. Some women cried at the sight of the "poor, half-starved, half-naked, hollow-eyed" men.[11] Many Texans wrote in their journals about how kind the Mexican women were, and the prisoners were "treated with marked humanity by all the better classes of the population."[12]

The Texans had been through rain and battle in what they were wearing, so some kind people gave them clothes. No one was in greater need than Bigfoot. His pants had worn completely out, and he had only his long shirt that went down to his knees. He later described his condition:

> ... my costume was not exactly a suitable one for a ballroom ... My hat had long since gone by the board, and in place of it my head was partially protected from the sun by a red cotton handkerchief wrapped around it somewhat in the fashion of a Turkish turban. I had but one shoe left, which was in a very dilapidated condition, and in lieu of the other a raw-hide sandal was strapped on my foot with leathern thongs.[13]

Two people treated the Texans with particular kindness. The first was an escaped slave named Noble, who the Texans said proved worthy of his name. He had run away from his owner somewhere on the Colorado River in Texas. Soon after the Texans were locked in jail, Noble came with provisions. He used all the money he had — several hundred dollars — to feed the starving prisoners.[14]

An Englishman who was living in Matamoros had known one of the prisoners, Major Oldham, when they were in Kentucky. The Englishman loaned Oldham $100 and advanced $2,000 dollars to the prisoners. He also gave $5 to each man who happened to be from Kentucky. There seemed to be an extraordinary number of men from Kentucky.[15]

The Texans, encouraged by their kind treatment, expected to go home soon, but they learned that the Mexican government, at the command of Santa Anna, was going to have them marched to Mexico City. Most of them did not realize what a terrible ordeal this would be. But John Day Morgan and the other Santa Fe men had made the march once before. They knew.

The Texans were transferred into the command of the hated General Canales, Ewen Cameron's enemy. General Ampudia, who all agreed had treated the men kindly, is said to have stayed awake all night worrying about the change of command, but it was out of his hands.

General Fisher and General Green were to be taken ahead of the other Texans and were to be executed if the Texan soldiers tried to escape. But when Fisher and Green visited the soldiers, they told Ewen Cameron to do whatever was necessary to get the volunteers back to Texas.

Whatever may be said about Fisher's poor judgment or Green's self-importance, they clearly did not put their personal safety above the welfare of their men.

CHAPTER 22

Texans Start for Mexico City

The Texans, in different groups, at different times, and at different places, began the long trek to Mexico City.

On January 12, 1843, General Fisher, General Green, and Adjutant-General Thomas W. Murray set out, lightly guarded, for Monterrey. General Ampudia also allowed them to take Dr. Shepherd and two aides. They chose Dan Henrie, who could serve as an interpreter, and old Sailing Master Samuel Lyons. Green pretended that Lyons was his personal body servant, and by doing this spared the old man many hardships. Fire eaters Billy Reese and Orlando Phelps were also with Green's group.

On January 14, 1843, Canales had the other Texans put in chains for their long march. General Ampudia intervened and ordered that the Texans' chains be removed. He also saw that John C. C.'s father was given a horse. Neither of these good acts lasted for long. As soon as the troops were at a distance from Ampudia, Asa's horse was taken away, and he and all the Texans were again put in chains.

In Matamoros

Six of the Texans were not well and were kept in Matamoros. Tender hearted John Day Morgan was kept behind to care for them.

General Ampudia had planned to send all the fire eaters

except John C. C. back home, but Santa Anna would not allow their return. He said that if these young men (Billy Reese, Orlando Phelps, Gilbert Brush, and Harvey Sellers) were released, they would return and fight Mexico again. Since he wasn't allowed to send the boys home, General Ampudia tried to at least spare them the suffering of the long march to Mexico City. Gilbert Brush and Harvey Sellers remained in Matamoros with John Day Morgan and the sick men. They were fortunate, for the time being, in having considerable freedom.[1]

Santa Anna (1794-1876)

Antonio López de Santa Anna Pérez de Lebrón was named president of Mexico five times, imprisoned three times, and exiled for life three times. Santa Anna was a *criollo*, or Mexican of European linage. He had limited education, and became a cadet in the Royalist, or Spanish, infantry when he was sixteen. At this time Mexico belonged to Spain, but was in continuous revolt. He spent the next five years fighting revolutionaries and keeping order among the Indian tribes. He was cited for bravery and steadily rose in rank. However, in 1821, he changed allegiance and joined the rebel forces against Spain. He became a brigadier general, but shifted his loyalties several times. This is often cited as an example of his disloyalty and emphasis on self interest. However, it is easy to see how a person whose youth was spent in battle would not hold clearly thought out and firm political views. This is particularly true since Mexico was in constant political chaos.

Furthermore, the Mexican class system created loyalty to social status rather than to nationality. Santa Anna's dynamic personality combined with his ability to put an army together quickly with little money, caused Mexico to call on him again and again. Although a good soldier and shrewd in sizing up situations and seizing power, he had little interest in the day to day running of the country. Typically, he would win a battle, be made president, then turn the responsibilities over to a subordinate and retire to his rural estate. He was prone to individual acts of generosity. Although he had children of his own, he adopted a poor boy, Guillermo Valle, and educated him. Guillermo became a lawyer and defended Santa Anna in some of his difficulties. Santa Anna fell from power in 1845 and was exiled to Havana, Cuba. He returned to power during the Mexican-American War, but was exiled again. He was later allowed to return to Mexico where he lived in retirement during his last years.

John C. C., living with General Ampudia and his kind family, was even more fortunate. With his father's permission, he had been enrolled in school in Matamoros under the name Juan Cristobal Colon Gil de Ampudia. John C. C. threw himself into his studies. This may have been a form of escape from his worries and confusion. If so, it was successful because he was seen to run about Matamoros "as gay as a lark."[2] During those days, he must have thought of Joseph Mendes, his adopted Mexican brother, who had divided loyalties. Only a few months earlier, John C. C.'s loyalties had been simple and clear. Now things were different. Mexicans had become his friends and protectors, as kind to him as he and his family had been to Joseph Mendes. Yet some of the Mexicans were oppressing his friends, his father, and his brother.

Fisher's and Green's Road to Saltillo

Because they were officers, General Fisher and General Green were spared the hardships of the common soldiers, as were their aides. In Monterrey, they stayed in the home of an army colonel and were entertained in a high style that was quite new to them. The colonel's daughters played the piano and the guitar. Fisher and Green were guests at lavish dinners along with Monterrey's most prominent citizens. They danced with the beautiful ladies who Green described as "winged creatures . . . with a bewitching, ethereal gossamer touch."[3]

It seems remarkable that prisoners would be invited to dances, but at that time, officers were treated with respect and could enjoy social occasions. The Mexican translator even acted as social guide and protected them against embarrassments. Green had been shrewd indeed to seize the position of second in command.

Smoking was stylish among the Mexican *señoritas*. At one of the elegant parties, Green's dancing partner offered him a cigarette lighted with the one she had been smoking. He was not a smoker and started to refuse the elegant flirtation, but his translator warned him that if he did not accept it, he would insult the lady. Green, therefore, felt obligated to smoke. He crossed his legs, looked up to the ceiling "with the little burning abhorrence" sticking to his lips, and tried to look sophisticated. He took several puffs and felt that he was having such great success, he would chance squeezing the smoke out through his nose. In this he failed, squeezing it instead into his "lungs and stomach, thus creating deadly nausea." He broke for the door "like a quarter-horse."[4] However, the diplomatic translator turned Green's grief into a compliment. He told the young lady that it was the first time Green had smoked and that he did it in compliment to her beauty. The lady was flattered.

But dinners and dances in Monterrey lasted only a short six days. Then, under guard by their Mexican escorts, Green, Fisher, and their aides rode on to Saltillo. They arrived on January 30, 1843, and were quartered in an infantry barracks. The men who had been kidnapped in San Antonio by General Woll were there. So, in different quarters, were Norman Woods and his eighteen-year-old nephew, Milvern Harrell.[5]

Norman Woods and Milvern Harrell's Road to Saltillo

Two months earlier, in November 1842, Norman Woods, Milvern Harrell, and Dawson prisoners John Higgerson, John MacCredae and W. D. Patterson had been kept behind at Presidio del Rio Grande. Patterson, MacCreadae, and Harrell attempted an escape which Harrell later recorded in detail. He wrote:

> As we were still suffering from our wounds, we were placed in a house at the Presidio del Rio Grande, just across the river on the Mexican side. Here we were guarded and kept confined for two months. Finally, we planned to make our escape, but gave it up, as we concluded that we could not cross the river. A Frenchman came in soon after, and

telling him of the plans we had entertained, he said that crossing the river would be easy, as it was low at that season. Encouraged by this, we again determined upon escaping.

Having noticed that the soldiers played cards a good deal, and satisfying ourselves that their guns were unloaded, one bright moonlight night, after the guard had passed the door, we slipped out and ran around the house toward the river. The ground was covered with rocks, and we fell several times. My uncle, Norman Woods, as he had not recovered from his wound, was easily retaken, but a man named Pattison, myself, and McReady ran on. We did not go directly to the river, which was only a mile or two distant, but ran up stream for ten or twelve miles, reaching it at about daylight. We looked for a shoaly place to cross, as we thought there the water would be shallow. As Pattison was the eldest of the three, we followed his advice. He selected a place where the river was narrow, and bent in toward the Texas side. A sandbar lay out in the water a little distance, and a high bluff arose on the opposite side. After wading past the sandbar, Pattison suddenly stepped into deep water, and swimming forward called us to come on, that we could swim over. The water was icy cold and we had been confined until we were weak. We had gone only a little distance when McReady called to us that he could go no further, and sank. Pattison and myself swam on. A jeans coat that Pattison had tied around him had slipped off, and he asked me to get it for him. I turned back for the coat, and taking it in my teeth, swam after him. On nearing the Texas bank, we got into a swift current and were washed rapidly down stream. Pattison called out to me that he could go no further, but must drown, and sank almost immediately. By this time I was completely exhausted, and was helpless in the current. Thinking every second would be the last, I was suddenly washed upon a rock in the river, and carried high upon it, the water being only about six inches over its surface. I stood up and stretched myself. It was sleeting now and I was almost frozen. I decided that I could not reach the Texas side, and knowing that I would freeze where I was, I went back to the Mexican side of the river. There was a long smooth beach where I reached the bank, and I ran up and down it for some time to warm myself and to loosen my joints, which had become stiff from being in the water so long.

Then leaving the river and going upon a hill to get my location, I saw a house in the distance, and I went toward it. A Mexican, seeing me approaching, came down to meet me. When he drew nearer, I recognized him as a Mexican I had known at San Antonio, and with whom we had traded. He came up and taking off his overcoat threw it around me. I went up to the house with him, where he had a big, bright fire in the chimney. He would not let me go near it, but had me to sit across the room from it, and would have me move up a little at a time. His wife brought in some hot coffee for me, and I thought it was the best I had ever tasted. After getting warm, I told them that I desired to lay down, as I was sleepy. A bed was prepared, and I slept from about 7 o'clock in the morning until 2 or 3 o'clock in the afternoon, and on awakening, I saw four Mexican soldiers in the room.

They had been scouring the country in search of us, and came to the house where I was. Of course they carried me back with them.[6]

This account was written for a newspaper when Harrell was sixty-five, some forty-seven years after the event.

After the attempted escape, in December of 1842, Norman Woods, Milvern Harrell, and John Higgerson were taken from Presidio to San Fernando, on their way to Saltillo. Norman Woods lost the handkerchief he used to cover the saber wounds on his head. Without even that slight protection from the winter cold, he fell so ill that he lay in bed in San Fernando for two months and would have surely died without Harrell's care.

They went to Saltillo on February 5, 1843. From there, on February 6, they were put on the road to San Luis Potosí with Fisher and Green's group.[7]

The Mier Men March to Saltillo

The common soldiers who were captured at Mier had

none of the pleasant times their officers, Fisher and Green, experienced. The soldiers were almost always hungry. Twice each day they were given a small piece of boiled beef in a pint of broth, a few grains of rice, a few beans, and a small piece of dry, stale bread. It was barely enough to keep them alive, but they refused to let their spirits sink. The most lighthearted time was in the evening before taps. The men made jokes and there was a general spirit of fun.[8]

When they got to Monterrey, General Canales turned the Texan prisoners over to Colonel Manuel Barragán, for the march from Monterrey to Saltillo. Colonel Barragán had only 100 cavalrymen and 100 infantrymen whereas General Canales had 1,000 cavalrymen and 500 infantrymen.[9] Moreover, Barragán's troops were not disciplined or well trained. Most of them had been taken from prisons and forced to bear arms. Colonel Barragán, well aware of the weakness of his force, soon managed to add another 100 infantrymen known as the "Red Caps."[10] The small size of the force gave the Texans ideas.

In Saltillo, one of the Mexican guards, in a mean-spirited gesture, threw an old infantryman's jacket at Bate Berry's feet. The jacket was a mass of tatters "that even a beggar would have thrown aside,"[11] but Berry picked it up. He saw that one sleeve was fairly sound, ripped it off, and hid it in his clothes. The murder of his brother, lying injured and helpless, burned in Berry's memory. He wanted revenge and was alert to anything that could possibly become a weapon, even an old sleeve.

CHAPTER 23

Texans Make a Break

At Hacienda de Salado

The volunteers crossed paths with their officers, General Fisher and General Green, at a way station called Haciendo de Salado. It was a stopping place for travelers going from Saltillo to San Luis Potosí. Although by policy the captured officers were quartered separately from their soldiers, some of the soldiers were allowed to visit Fisher and Green. They conferred. Should the soldiers break out? Their escape would mean death to Fisher and Green, who nevertheless urged their men to seize any opportunity that might come their way.

A cold wind swept down from the sierras. The prisoners, who were confined in a corral, were given a small quantity of wood. John Rufus Alexander made a little fire, sat beside it, and talked with Dr. Richard F. Brenham, thirty-three. Brenham, originally from Kentucky, had practiced medicine in Austin. He had been on the Santa Fe Expedition. He felt sure that he would be executed when they got to Mexico City since the terms of his release were that he would be shot if he ever again took up arms against Mexico. Brenham thought his best alternative was to escape. Alexander didn't believe a break would succeed. They were about 200 miles from Texas, and he thought they were too deep into Mexico. However, he said if the other men decided to try, he would join them.

Captain Reese, thirty-three, brother of fire eater Billy Reese, strongly opposed the escape. He had fought heroically at Mier, had staunchly opposed surrender, and had advocated escape earlier. But now he thought that they were too far from the Texas border. He said the attempt should have been made sooner, and that now they were sure to be caught. "You have sinned away your days of grace," he told the others. "What was courage and wisdom on the Rio Grande would be madness and weakness here."[1]

Such comments irritated Captain Ewen Cameron. He was determined to make the break even if he had to do it "all alone and single-handed."[2]

The charismatic Cameron was able to inspire men to follow him simply by the strength of his powerful personality. In this case, however, General Green had given him information to support his position—the roads leading to the towns along the Rio Grande were not guarded.

Even so, a vote showed that only about a third of the 214 prisoners wanted to make the attempt, but that third was so eager to escape that they persuaded most of the others to join them. They would make their break in the morning when the horses were in from grazing and available for capture.

They debated making Dr. Brenham their leader but feared "that his impetuous daring and ardent feelings would urge him into measures beyond prudence."[3] Considering the swashbuckling standards of the Mier men, it is hard to imagine a person they would see as too impetuous and imprudent.

Captain Cameron was chosen as leader. He was certainly brave—some would call him reckless—but he was seen as more cautious and wise than Brenham. Cameron told the men that they must not kill any more Mexican soldiers than was necessary. The sick, the wounded, and the few who were still unwilling to chance the break would be put in danger if the others killed ruthlessly.

Excited at the thought of breaking free, some of the Texans frolicked far into the night, dancing and singing. When the Mexicans asked why they were in such high spirits, the Texans answered that they were celebrating St. Valentine's Day, four days away. "The men lay down to rest, resolved that the morning's sun would shine upon free men or set on their graves."[4]

Outside the corral's rock fence, where the whole forces' muskets were stacked, only two guards watched the gate. Perhaps the Mexicans, like many of the Texans, thought they were now too far from the border for escape to be reasonable.

The Escape

On the morning of February 11, 1843, unknown to the rest of the Texans, Fisher, Green, and their aides, under the guard of Captain Romano, left Hacienda de Salado for Mexico City.

The Texans would strike while the Mexicans were eating breakfast. Pots of rice were brought in for the prisoners. The Texans peered watchfully from under the slouched brims of their hats as they ate. Captain Cameron dipped his gourd into the rice, then moved near the door. Outside in the courtyard, the Mexican soldiers began to prepare their own meal. The Texans watched, tensed for Cameron's signal.

Cameron threw his hat in the air.

The Texans raised a yell.

The fight was on.

A volley of rocks knocked several Mexicans from their positions on the walls. At the gate, "The Lionlike Cameron" placed a hand upon the chest of each sentinel, hurled them far away "as the whirlwind scatters chaff," and ran out. The Texans poured through after their leader, squeezing through the narrow gate.[5] In their rush, they knocked Mexican soldiers to the ground and trampled them. Unable to stop the Texan stampede, the Mexicans turned and ran.

About fifty cavalrymen under Colonel Barragán galloped onto the plain. Texans and Mexicans ran for the same guns. They fought hand to hand. The Texans had endured an difficult trip, and had been kept half starved so that they would be weak and manageable, but they had the advantage in size and strength, and they soon had the advantage of weapons. After the first discharge, the Texans rushed among the Mexicans using their guns as clubs. Some Mexican soldiers took refuge in nearby buildings, firing on the Texans from there. Colonel Barragán galloped toward them to join the battle.

John Rufus Alexander grabbed a musket, but was disappointed to find that it wasn't loaded. "The [Mexican] infantry . . . tried to surrender, but for a time no stop could be put to the slaughter. Finally, the men listened to Cameron, who went among the men and begged for the lives of the disarmed guards. . . . Many Mexicans lay dead on every side, while others were moaning with broken heads and gunshot wounds."[6]

Bigfoot Wallace tried to disarm an infantryman who had just fired. The Mexican had a bayonet attached to his musket and thrust it at Bigfoot. He seized it. They struggled. At last the bayonet came off in Bigfoot's hands. Another Texan grabbed the gun. "The Mexican fell to his knees, held up his hands, and begged for mercy."[7] Bigfoot granted it.

Young George Washington Trahern grabbed a guard's musket. The guard fired at him. The bullet hit the top of Trahern's hand and set his clothes on fire.[8]

Bate Berry put a round stone that weighed about a pound in the old coat sleeve he had hidden away. He swung it, and brained two soldiers.[9]

Dr. Brenham rushed at a Mexican soldier. The Mexican fell to the ground, and his gun fell toward Brenham, who ran into it. The bayonet passed through Brenham's body and killed him.[10]

Mexican Lieutenant Barragán, son of Colonel Barragán, fought valiantly. Six Texans armed with fixed bayonets demanded that he yield. "His saber made such rapid movements that it was hardly visible."[11] He was backed against a wall, but he refused to surrender except to an officer. To do so would have been to dishonor his rank and class. Death was preferable.

Someone told Bigfoot Wallace to get a loaded gun and shoot young Barragán. Bigfoot wouldn't do it. He said such a brave man should be spared. At last, Lieutenant Barragán surrendered his sword to Captain Cameron. Then "with a proud look the Mexican stepped back and folded his arms."[12]

CHAPTER 24

Thomas Jefferson Green Uses Suasion

Captain Romano and his little band of seven Texan prisoners, including Fisher and Green, were less than a mile from Hacienda de Salado when they heard sounds of gunfire. Captain Romano halted the prisoners and ordered Lieutenant Arredondo and fifteen men to go back and find out what the shooting was about. The rest of the group went on at a full gallop, the guards riding on each side of the Texans, lances ready. They had gone only about 100 yards when they halted on a small knoll. The Texans were ordered to dismount. Soon the sounds of firing stopped and shouts of "Hurrah for Texas!" and "To hell with Mexico!" reached their ears. Fisher and Green knew the escaping prisoners were winning, and they began to cheer.

Lieutenant Arredondo galloped up the knoll with a message from Colonel Barragán. He told Romano to execute Fisher, Green and their aides and then return to help at Hacienda de Salado.

Calmly, Green asked Romano if he were not bound to obey the orders of Jose Maria Ortega, Governor of Nuevo León, who had commanded him to escort them to Mexico City. Surely, he argued, this order should rank above Barragán's order. Green added that he had assumed they were in the hands of a gentleman and a soldier, not a murderer.

Romano lowered his eyes to the pommel of his saddle and thought about Green's remarks. Then he raised himself in his stirrups and clapped his hand on his bosom. He declared that he was a gentleman and a soldier and would carry out the orders of Governor Ortega. He sent some soldiers back to help Barragán. Then his reduced force and their Texan prisoners turned their horses' heads toward Mexico City.[1]

Green's quick thinking and clever appeal to rank, class, and honor saved their lives.

CHAPTER 25

After the Battle at Hacienda de Salado

Eighteen Texans stayed behind at Hacienda de Salado. Five of them had been wounded in the escape.[1] Norman Woods was too sick to go, and his nephew, Milvern Harrell, stayed to take care of him.

Nine Texans who opposed the break also stayed behind. Although Captain Reese had been against it, he fought zealously. He would have fled with the escaping Texans, but he didn't want his young brother, fire eater Billy Reese, to take that risk. Billy had also fought valiantly and when his brother tried to persuade him to stay behind, he refused. He yielded only when Captain Reese vowed to stay with him.

On the other hand, fire eater Orlando Phelps didn't take part in the fighting, but eagerly took part in the escape. He grabbed a horse and galloped away, refusing to even carry a gun.[2]

The Texans took time in their escape to bury their five slain comrades.[3] They released the Mexican prisoners after they promised that the wounded Texans would be cared for. Then they gathered provisions and horses and were off. They had done more than escape; they had defeated their captors.

The 191 Texans had ninety mules and horses, 160 muskets and carbines, three mule loads of ammunition, and $1,400 in silver coin.[4]

After they had gone only half a mile north of Hacienda de Salado, Colonel Barragán and a small party of soldiers caught up with them. He told Captain Cameron that if the Texans would surrender, they would be treated kindly and would not be punished. He said that it would be impossible for them to make it safely to the Rio Grande.

Cameron turned a deaf ear to those pleas, but because of Colonel Barragán's humane treatment of the Texans when they were under his guard, he ordered that Barragán's personal horse and equipment be returned to him. Cameron also asked Barragán to take care of the wounded, and Barragán promised that he would.[5]

Bigfoot Wallace described Barragán as a "clever fellow and a gentleman although he had the misfortune to be born a Mexican."[6]

The Texans were on their way. They sang and "scared with their jovial echoes the startled wild-bird from its perch."[7] They "went at a trot the whole time, those on foot keeping up with the horsemen at the gait until exhausted, when they would take their turn in riding."[8] Although Barragán's cavalry did not attempt to stop the Texans, they did trail them, and they sent frequent smoke signals.

By daybreak the Texans had traveled an incredible seventy miles. They came to the Monclovia Road and turned north toward the Rio Grande. At this time the fleeing Texans were the best armed force between Saltillo and the Rio Grande.

Dr. John Cameron rode to meet them. He was a relative of Ewen Cameron and had a ranch in Mexico.[9] He gave them clear directions and told them at which ranches they could expect hospitality, at which ones, hostility. With this information and the guide Dr. Cameron offered to give them, the Texans should have had a quick and easy journey to Texas, but instead, they made a fatal and shockingly stupid decision. They decided to take to the mountains.

There was no good reason for making such a decision. Hunger and hardship must have clouded the Texans' judgment, which was poor enough at best. Some of them thought that Dr. John Cameron was deceiving them, though they had no evidence. Indeed, the things he had told them proved true thus far, but they were convinced that he was sending them into Mexican hands. As usual, there was disagreement between the men of most influence. Captain G. W. Pierson and Captain William M. Eastland were determined to take to the mountains. Ewen Cameron, beloved leader and master of the escape, could not influence the men to follow him. Since the headstrong Texans would not be led, Cameron went with them. He hoped to later bring them back to the Monclovia road. Cameron's loyalty to the foolish and unruly Texans never wavered. Perhaps this loyalty, like cattle raiding, was part of the deeply ingrained culture of the Scottish clan.

So all the escaped Texans left the clear, straight road and went into the uncharted mountains.

CHAPTER 26

In the Mountains

Off the Road

The mountains were the harsh and barren Sierra de la Paila. The Texans climbed all day without finding water. They met steep cliffs and granite walls. There was no grass for the animals, and the horses and mules could barely walk on the sharp rocks. Many were injured.

The Texans slept on the bare mountain side. The next morning, they saw that they would have to abandon the horses and mules. They had gone too far, or were too lost, to return to the road as Cameron had hoped. They were afraid to waste their ammunition, so they killed the mules and horses by stabbing them in their hearts.

"It was a sad, heart-rending ordeal. . . . These patient animals had borne us thus far, and even now, while we were planning their destruction in their famished condition, their gentle lustrous eyes were turned upon us appealingly for relief."[1]

"Men wept as they stuck knives into the faithful beasts that looked at them with astonished eyes."[2] Bigfoot Wallace said that his horse looked "so knowingly and pleading out of his sunken hollow eyes, that my heart failed me entirely, and my comrade, who was not so 'squeamish,' had to play the role of executioner."[3] Some of the men drank the animals' blood. They roasted the flesh over small brush fires and made rough sandals out of parts of the saddles.

When they resumed their climb and reached the summit of the mountain, they saw that crest after barren crest lay in front of them. Some men chose to stop by the wayside and wait to be recaptured. Later, others stopped because they were too weak to carry on.

The Texans had a little horse meat, but their throats were too dry to swallow it. They suffered more from thirst than hunger. They scratched in the shade of bushes trying to find cool earth to put on their throats and stomachs. Their tongues were so parched and swollen that they couldn't close their mouths. Some of them chewed cactus leaves, but that only made them sick. Some drank the juice of the maguey plant, which they found pleasant tasting, but which later made their mouths burn. The skin peeled off wherever the juice had touched, and sores soon formed.

Finally, they broke into groups, hoping one group would find water and signal with a fire. The largest group was Captain Cameron's, which had about eighty-five men. Other groups had from two to ten men. Men dropped their weapons as they stumbled on, casting away muskets, cartridges, machetes. They even threw away their silver coins "as a child would sail a flat stone."[4]

Some wandered in their minds, and prayed, or cursed, or sang. Bigfoot recorded that one man, "crazy as a bed-bug" and staggering as he walked, sang cheerily in a faint voice, "Who'll be king but Charlie."[5]

General Francisco Mejia, the governor of Coahuila, assembled a local militia to go after the Texans. He contacted Jose Maria Ortega, the governor of Nuevo León, who also raised a force. The combined total was 750 men. They were stationed at places where the Texans would be likely to come out of the mountains.

Individual Experiences

George Trahern. Many stories of the Texans' individual experiences have been recorded. George Washington Trahern, whose clothes were set on fire in the escape, hadn't had a drink for six days when an old Mexican picked him up like he was a child and carried him to water. Trahern could take a thorn and pierce his leg and not draw a drop of blood. He said that in that stage a man would walk along and draw wind like he was sucking water, and look like death.[6]

James Glasscock. James A. Glasscock had to betray his friends in order to save them. After the Texans split up into small groups, he and William H. Van Horn walked for two days without finding water. On the third day, they saw smoke. They hoped the smoke was a signal from some other Texans who had found water. Their spirits lifted. Instead, it came from the smoldering of a burned prairie. There were neither people nor water there. Later, John Thomas Dillon, who had been walking alone, joined Glasscock and Van Horn. All three were terribly weak. Glasscock, the strongest of the three, pounded the leaves of a maguey plant with a stone for the little moisture the leaves would yield.

Again the men saw smoke and went toward it. This time they found a recent campsite, but again found no water. The next day Van Horn and Dillon, who by now could barely walk, lay in the shade of an overhanging rock while Glasscock, taking a gourd to use as a canteen, went to search for water. In the distance, he saw some bulrushes, and he knew that there would likely be water where that plant grew, but before Glasscock reached the bulrushes, he was captured. He knew his friends would die if they did not have water soon, so he told the Mexicans where they were. The Mexicans took Glasscock to a ranch where he had his first drink in six days, and in a couple of hours, Van Horn and Dillon were brought in.

Captain Claudius Buster and Private John Toops. Captain Claudius Buster, who had coolly ordered his men to kneel and get out of the Mexican line of fire in the battle of Mier, had joined Captain Ewen Cameron's group. With him were Private John Toops and other men of Company D, Captain Buster's command. On Friday, February 17, Cameron's group started early, determined to cover as much ground as possible before the heat of the day. Toops and some other men scouted for water and found a few gallons three miles from the group. In spite of their need for water, the group decided to push on without delay. Toops drank his fill and carried a gourdful to Captain Buster. Buster took one mouthful and distributed the rest among his men.[7]

Later, Buster and Toops were separated from Cameron's group and weren't able to find them. Buster said that he was eight days without water. His tongue was swollen so that he couldn't talk, and he could barely walk. When he and Toops came to a bed of dry sand in a cool hollow where there had been water in wet seasons, they scratched off the crust and wallowed like hogs to cool themselves.[8]

Luckily they came on a rock filled with rain water. They later became so weak that they could hardly stay awake when they paused for rest. They would have died, but they came upon an ox. They killed the animal and drank the blood, but they didn't have anything to butcher it with. The sharpest thing they had was the flint of Buster's musket. With that, they managed to cut out the liver. They roasted and ate it. This gave them strength to go on.

Soon afterward they found some ranch houses. The *rancheros* treated them kindly. Buster and Toops still had their part of the silver from Salado. With it they bought supplies and moved on toward Laredo. They made it across the mountains and all the way to the Rio Grande about thirty miles above Laredo.

They were nearly safe, but they needed to eat before they tried to cross the river. They walked along the bank until they came to some deserted ranch quarters. They found the warm remains of a campfire and some scraps of food. This would be their meal. They started eating, but before they finished ten Mexican cavalrymen galloped up. Buster and Toops were caught.

Their hands and feet were tied; then they were placed on their backs and tied together. Sentinels stood over them with orders to shoot them if they moved. They were kept a few days near Laredo, then were sent to Guerrero, then Monterrey, and then Saltillo.

William Oldham. Other men, crazed with thirst, wandered off from Cameron's group. Mexicans picked them up here and there. William Oldham and Thomas A. Thompson were trailing in the rear, too weak to keep up with the others. They spotted a Mexican camp. Thompson said there must be water in the camp, and he was going to get it. Oldham told him that was too dangerous, but Thompson wouldn't listen. He gave Oldham his gun and ammunition, they shook hands, and Thompson left for the Mexican camp.

When daylight came, Oldham concealed himself in a deep gully and stayed there all day. About sundown a large body of Mexican cavalry passed nearby. Oldham climbed a mountain to get away from them and stumbled onto water. He drank, then kept going until he fell from exhaustion. He went to sleep where he fell, and in the morning, he was awakened by a bird's song. When he opened his eyes, he saw that a bird was sitting on his breast "almost splitting his little throat with his morning song."[9] Oldham felt that this was a good omen. He took courage and went on.

The various stories of the fearlessness of the wildlife indicate that few humans had passed that way. It was wild country, indeed.

Dreams. Some of the Texans later spoke of their dreams when they were lost. Bigfoot Wallace said rippling brooks and gushing streams haunted a thirsty dreamer's mind, but when the dreamer approached to drink, horrible shapes would "gibber and moan"[10] and frighten him away. Bigfoot himself dreamed of a spring he had known in Virginia as a boy. In his dream, he tried repeatedly to drink from it, but something would always prevent his placing his lips on the mossy spot. Years later he returned to Virginia and to the spring. Although he was not at all thirsty, he drank there. It was a symbolic victory.

John Rufus Alexander, who, with some friends, broke off from Cameron, later described a dream he had on his fourth day without water. He saw himself at a great banquet. Family and friends offered him all kinds of delicious dishes, but he pushed the food aside and asked for water. They gave it to him, but as he drank each jar, his thirst became stronger. No one at the banquet seemed in the least surprised.[11]

When Alexander awoke, he and some friends again began to search for water. Alexander dragged himself down the mountain. Like a miracle, he found a waterfall gushing from a rock.

John Rufus Alexander and William Oldham. The next day, Alexander and his companions went north, but they didn't find any more water. One by one, suffering men left the group and went off alone. Alexander's friend, John L. Cash, scouted an arroyo. When Alexander got to the place where they were supposed to meet, Cash was nowhere to be found. Alexander and the others called, but he didn't answer. Finally they had to move on, their hearts heavy. Alexander said, "I loved Cash, and it grieved me to lose him in that impossible wilderness."[12]

As they toiled on, they noticed that "someone was dogging their steps." A voice called out, "Boys, where are you?" It was Major Oldham. He was overjoyed to get back in "good but very forlorn" company.[13] Alexander and Oldham vowed to stay together. Others soon drifted off alone or in pairs. At last, Alexander and Oldham were the only ones left. They struggled on.

Oldham had the good luck to find a beehive. He used his bayonet to rob it, but he was severely stung, and Alexander said Oldham "came near to dying that night."[14] When he recovered, Oldham removed his goatskin leggings, tied the lower ends, revisited the bee cave, and filled them with honey.

Soon afterward, Alexander fell sick with a raging fever, and Oldham took care of him. Alexander felt sure he was going to die, and he begged Oldham to leave him and try to survive himself. Oldham reminded Alexander that they had made a vow to stay together. He stayed and nursed Alexander. Oldham even managed to make a broth from the balmony plant, which was used as a remedy for many ailments in Texas at that time.[15] Alexander drank the broth, and though he said the effect was nearly as fierce as the disease, he got better.[16]

One day they happened onto a herdsman's shanty. No one was there, so they made themselves at home. They found a mug of goat's milk, a few tortillas, some shelled corn, and some mutton suet which they "promptly transferred to the department of the interior."[17]

Alexander found a pair of tanned goat skin pants that had the waistband missing. His own pants were in tatters except for the waistband which was in good condition. So he put the new pants, which fit him perfectly, onto his old waistband and "went forth as proud as any boy with his first breeches."[18] That they were leather was a real bonus since that offered good protection from thorns and cactus needles.

Alexander didn't mention how Oldham was faring since he had used his leggings for honey. Evidently they had managed to each keep some possessions because when Oldham and Alexander crossed a river, the water was waist deep on the tall Alexander, and he made two trips carrying their things, and then went back to help Oldham.

At last, the friends made it to the banks of the Rio Grande. There they found a stock pen and used the wood to make a raft. Even when they got across, they were not safe. The people of Laredo had not forgotten the sack of their town, and their militia was watching for the Texans. Alexander and Oldham had to skirt around the town through the scrub brush.

In April, two months after they escaped from Salado, Alexander and Oldham limped into San Antonio.[19] Alexander said that more uncouth and more forlorn looking men had never entered the plaza. People looked at them in amazement; but when they learned who the wretched wanderers were, they threw their homes open to them, and gave them clothing, saddles, bridles, and horses.[20]

Alexander and Oldham were fortunate indeed. Of the 191 men who escaped from Hacienda de Salado, only six arrived home to Texas.[21]

CHAPTER 27

Recapture

Picking Up Texans

Some of the Mexican soldiers found an easy way to catch escaped Texans. They located water, made themselves comfortable beside it, and waited for the thirsty escapees to come to them. John Taney, who was a great whistler and who had whistled like a fife when the Texans marched into Mier, was drawn to the water like a thirsty animal. When he saw the Mexicans there, he hid behind some scrub brush. A soldier recognized him and called, "Ah! Mr. Whistler, how do you do?"[1]

Other groups of escaped Texans were picked up and were taken to Boca de los Tres Rios. They waited there while more of their comrades were rounded up. All of them were severely changed by the eleven days in the mountains. Their beards and hair were rough, uncombed, and matted, and their eyes glared wildly from their pinched faces.

Cameron Is Caught

By February 18, Cameron's group in the mountains had shrunk from eighty-five to fifty wretched men, including old Asa Hill. They saw smoke rising from a fire and staggered toward it, thinking it was a signal that some of their group had found water. Instead, they found themselves in a Mexican camp. Even then, Cameron tried to bargain. He said they would lay down their few weapons in return for being treated like prisoners of war. But the Mexicans made no promises, and the Texans had no choice. They needed water.

Cameron's "Cowboys," desperate for a drink, learned that their captors didn't have water. ". . . The rascals had been without water two days themselves."[2] The Mexicans sent men to the nearest water hole twelve miles away, and the Texans were made to lie near the smoldering camp fires until daylight.

Cameron's captive cowboys arrived at Paso de Benado the next day. The men were tied up but were treated mercifully. They were given plenty of beef and corn to eat. In a gesture of mistaken kindness, two men had been allowed to drink all the water they wanted. They died a few hours later. After that, the Mexicans only let the Texans drink small amounts at a time until their strength returned. Later some of the Texans expressed appreciation for the soldiers' careful rationing of the water.

Bigfoot Wallace, however, wouldn't settle for just a cup of water. He noticed a big gourd hanging from a horseman's saddle. It was his own gourd that had been taken away from him at Mier. Bigfoot said in Spanish, "That is my gourd. Give it up."

The Mexican soldier said, "*Probrecito*,"[3] and handed the gourd to him. Bigfoot upended it and started guzzling water. Another Texan, Tom Davis, ran up to him and said, "Give me some, Foot."[4]

But Bigfoot wouldn't turn the gourd loose. Davis tried to pull it away from Bigfoot's mouth, and several soldiers danced around Bigfoot, reaching for the gourd, but no one could grab it. Bigfoot was too tall. He drank a gallon of water and fell down in a dead sleep. He didn't move all night, and the soldiers thought he'd never wake again, but the next day he was fine.

Headed Back in Chains

William Thompson bound up his leg and pretended to be too lame to walk. The guard believed him and gave him a horse. Bigfoot knew Thompson was faking, but he wasn't inclined to tell.

After three days, all but fifty of the escaped Texans had been found. They began the march south toward Saltillo, and more Texans were picked up every day. The prisoners didn't have blankets. They endured hot days and cold nights. Some of them didn't even have shoes, and their feet bled "as they crippled over the stones that gashed them at every step."[5] Some were so weak they had to ride on mules, but the Mexicans feared another escape. They tied the men's wrists with leather thongs that scraped and cut their skin. Some men managed to untie themselves, but then the Mexicans beat them. They later replaced the leather thongs with iron handcuffs, but the handcuffs rubbed away the flesh and made the men's arms swell and turn black.

On February 21, the Mexican troops made a triumphal entry into Saltillo with their wretched prisoners. It was attended by a crowd of thousands. In preparation for the great event, the Texans were allowed to wash their faces. This was the first time they had washed since they slaughtered their horses.

Back in Saltillo, Captain Buster and John Toops were put in the state prison with men who had committed minor crimes. The room was so crowded that Buster felt suffocated. He called to the jailer and told him he couldn't stand to be in that room, and the jailer put him and Toops in a room with no roof. They could breathe there, but at night they were locked in with hardened criminals—those who had "committed the most heinous offenses."[6]

One of the Mexican prisoners had painted a picture of a devil on the wall. Captain Buster borrowed the man's paint and added a stake and chain. Then he wrote, "Chained for 1,000 years." When the new governor, General Biscinia, came to Saltillo and visited the prison, the picture caught his attention. "Who chained the devil?"[7] he asked.

Toops was pointed out, and with an interpreter Toops and the governor had a long talk. Toops took advantage of the moment and protested his treatment. He said he was a prisoner of war, not a convict. The governor agreed with him and had both Buster and Toops taken out of the prison and put into soldier's quarters. When Santa Anna ordered that all the Texan prisoners be sent to Mexico City, General Biscinia gave Buster and Toops a horse. Toops said Biscinia was the best friend he found in Mexico.

CHAPTER 28

The Black Bean Episode

"Shoot the Texans!"

The recaptured Texans stayed in the Saltillo jail for three weeks. Their destinies lay in hands 800 miles south in Mexico City, and communication was slow. At this time, Santa Anna was in semi-retirement in Veracruz. He had left General Nicolas Bravo in charge in Mexico City. Bravo had received news of the escape at Salado and sent word to Saltillo that the Texan escapees should be shot.

Mejia Refuses

General Mejia, showing himself to be a gentleman and a man of character, refused to carry out the order and resigned. This would only have given the Texans a few more days of life, except that Britain and the U.S. put diplomatic pressure on Mexico. The Republic of Texas could not itself exert such pressure since, although it had international recognition as a nation, it did not have diplomatic relations with Mexico. As far as Mexico was concerned, Texas was one of its rebel provinces.

"Decimate Them!"

Santa Anna felt that the deaths of the five Mexican soldiers during the escape from Hacienda de Salado demanded severe punishment. In what he considered an act of mercy, he changed the order that all the Texan captives be killed. Instead, he ordered that they be decimated — every tenth man should be shot. They would be chosen by lottery.

Santa Anna's command highlights the difference in the cultures and belief systems of the two countries at that time. The *diezmo* was a fairly common military punishment in Mexico and was long established under Spanish military law, but Anglos were shocked at such an order. To the Mexicans, killing one man out of ten was clearly better than killing them all, and the fairest way to choose was by random chance. To the Texans, gambling with men's lives was hideous.

On March 25, 1843, the Texans were manacled two by two and marched from Saltillo back to Hacienda de Salado where, six weeks earlier, they had made their glorious escape.

The Texans knew that General Mejia had resigned, but they had no idea of Santa Anna's new order. Nature, unlike the men, seemed to know of the horror ahead. The day was

---

Decimation

During the Mexican revolution of 1810, there were two instances of decimation, one in Guanajuato and the other in Guadalajara. Mexico was divided sharply by race and class, and there was no sense of unity based on simply being born in Mexico. General Calleja, who was loyal to Spain, ordered the decimation of all Indian and half-Indian people in Guanajuato. He erected a gallows in the plaza and one man in every ten, chosen by lot, was hanged. Their only crime was their Indian blood. In return, Miguel Hidalgo's army at Guadalajara carried out its own decimation of the Spaniards, who were marched outside the city and strangled. Their only crime was that they were of Spanish descent.

Mexico is still made up of three major groups: Creoles (people of Spanish descent), Mestizos (people of mixed Spanish and Indian descent), and pure indigenous Indians. Social ranking has been lessened, but it still exists, with Creoles at the top, Indians at the bottom.

clear and warm, but as the men neared Hacienda de Salado, the sky darkened, the wind howled, and a dust storm hit. The men could only see a few feet in front of them as they fought their way forward, leaning into the wind. Every man who still had a hat grabbed it with his free hand. When they got to Hacienda de Salado, they rushed, staggering, to a shed alongside the outer wall.

The prisoners saw several Mexicans digging a ditch. Henry Whaling, who had scolded Bigfoot for missing a shot in the first fight near San Antonio, now said to Bigfoot, "That ditch is for us."[1]

The Black Beans

Colonel Domingo Huerta had the men brought into the courtyard. Captive Alfred Thurmond had to act as interpreter and tell his comrades that every tenth man was to be shot. They looked at him in disbelieving silence. There were 176 men remaining of the 191 who had fled Hacienda de Salado. That meant that seventeen men would be shot.

A Mexican officer crossed the courtyard carrying a clay jar that tapered both at top and bottom "something like a tenpin."[2] The officer put the jar on the low wall before the Colonel and poured in 159 white beans, scattered 17 black beans over the top, and covered the jar with a cloth. The officers were to draw first; then the men were to draw in alphabetical order. The men who drew black beans would be shot.

Captain Cameron, who was manacled to Colonel William P. Morrow, stepped forward. "Well, boys, we have to draw, let's be at it,"[3] he said. With near superhuman restraint, he did not add that he had told them not to go into the mountains.

Morrow had watched the Mexican drop the black beans on top. He whispered, "Dip deep, Captain."[4]

Cameron pushed through toward the bottom of the jar and got a white bean. A soldier took it and laid it on the stone wall. The Mexican officers looked disappointed; they wanted

Cameron most of all. He had become a symbol of Texan resistance.

One by one the other officers drew: Colonel William F. Wilson, Captain William Ryan, Quartermaster Judge F. M. Gibson, and Captain William M. Eastland.

Captain Eastland was handcuffed to nineteen-year-old diarist Israel Canfield, who recorded the incident in detail. Eastland was the first to draw a black bean. He maintained dignity as his chains were struck off, and he gave his money to his brother-in-law, Robert Smith. Shockingly, Smith shouted that he had "made a raise."[5] In contrast, Eastland told his comrades, "For my country I have offered all my earthly aspiration and for it now I lay down my life. I never have feared death nor do I now."[6]

The soldiers drew next. When a soldier drew a black bean, he was unchained from his comrade and chained to a man in the death line. Sometimes two chained together would both draw death beans and would move together to the fatal line. Some of the men joked about their condition. One said, "Boys, this beats raffling all to pieces."[7]

Another joked, "This is the tallest gambling scrape I was ever in."

Robert Beard was too sick and exhausted to even stand. His brother, William, managed to bring him a cup of water.

Cameron: Rebel or Patriot? Thief or Raider?

From the Mexican viewpoint, Ewen Cameron was a dangerous rebel, mercenary, cattle thief, and gang leader. They had reason to think so. Cameron had fought in the Texas rebellion; he fought again in the failed Mexican Federalist attempt to overthrow the government; and he had led many cattle raids on law-abiding Mexican ranches. The Texans didn't consider him a cattle thief because, unlike many, he only took cattle from the Mexican ranchers, and the Texans thought that they were entitled to cattle owned by Mexicans since the Mexican army took Anglo cattle. To a Scot, like Ewen Cameron, border cattle raiding was a tradition. Soldiering for hire was an honorable occupation. None of these arguments carried much weight with his captors.

Robert said, "Brother, if you draw a black bean, I'll take your place; I want to die."

William answered, "No! I will keep my own place."[8]

The Mexicans would not have allowed switching in any event. They made the men draw alphabetically and kept a strict record.

One of the soldiers to draw a black bean was John Rufus Alexander's friend, Cash, who Alexander had feared was dead but who had actually been picked up when he went scouting the arroyo. Major James Cocke also drew a black bean. He held it up, and with a smile of contempt, said, "Boys, I told you so; I never failed in my life to draw a prize." To Quartermaster Judge Gibson, he said, "Well, Judge, say to my friends that I died in grace."

Quartermaster Gibson cried for Cocke.

On seeing Gibson's tears, Cocke said lightly, "They only rob me of forty years."[9]

Then, knowing that his body would be stripped after his death, he took off his outer clothes, gave them to his friends, and died in his underwear.[10]

Jolly little Henry Whaling drew a black bean. He would not let even death crush his spirit. It was said that he wore as bright a look as ever lighted man's countenance.

Whaling said, "Well, they don't make much off me, anyhow, for I know I have killed twenty-five of the yellow-bellies."[11] Then he demanded dinner. He had been hungry a long time, and he said, "I do not want to starve and be shot too."[12] The Mexicans honored his request. The cooks served mutton stew and beans and double rations were given to all the condemned men. Whaling was one of the few with appetite. He ate heartily, and smoked a last cigar. In twenty minutes, he was "launched into eternity."[13]

On drawing a black bean, a man named Torrey said, "I am perfectly willing to meet my fate. I fought for the glory of my country, and for her glory I am willing to die." On hearing this, J. L. Jones spoke to the interpreter. "Tell the officer to look upon men who are not afraid to die for their country."[14]

132 Mier Men

Torrey pointed out to the officer that his family had raised and educated a Mexican boy who had been captured at the Battle of San Jacinto—"and this is our requittal."[15]

Edward Este showed the "coolest indifference to his fate"[16] and said he would rather be shot than dragged along as they were.

Luckily, John Taney, the whistler, drew a white bean. So did John C. C.'s father, old Asa Hill. When it was "Talking" Bill Moore's turn to draw, he said, "Boys, I had rather draw for a Spanish horse and lose him." But he drew a white bean, also.[17]

Bigfoot Wallace was one of the last men to draw. When it came his turn, the man holding the jar was amazed at the size of Bigfoot's hand. He held it up for the other Mexicans to marvel at, and he taunted Bigfoot. But Bigfoot squeezed his huge hand down into the narrow neck of the jar, picked up two beans and felt them. He had noticed that the black beans were a little larger than the white ones. He pulled out the smaller one. It wasn't either black or white, but Huerta himself took it from Wallace and called the color white.[18] Either Huerta's kindness or Bigfoot's charm, or both, saved him.

Some of the Mexican officers also seemed to be saddened by the dreadful orders they had to carry out, but some took bets as at a sporting event, and others taunted the Texans. One particularly cruel and obnoxious officer sarcastically mimicked sympathy. If a man drew a black bean, he would say, "Better luck next time."[19]

There was only one of the Texans who was struck with fear and could not maintain dignity. On being told of the drawing, he wrung his hands and moaned. He said that he was sure to draw a black bean. When his name was called, he refused to move until a file of Mexican soldiers shoved him forward and forced his hand into the jar. They told him if he took more than one bean he would be shot. He was so slow that a Mexican officer pricked him severely with his sword to make him withdraw his hand from the jar. He drew a black bean. From that moment, though he turned deadly pale, he never said another word of complaint. Bigfoot Wallace said, "I pitied him from the bottom of my heart."[20]

Wallace told about an Irishman's drawing a bean. When the Irishman stuck his hand in the jar, there were so few beans that he jerked his hand out empty, and in his strong Irish accent, began to complain. He said the Mexicans were deceiving him to his destruction. He said he wouldn't draw because it wasn't fair. Other men been given a chance to pick and choose, but he hadn't. The Mexicans told him he would have to draw. He said they were "after murdering" him and called them "indecent bastards"[21] and "baboon faces."[22] He was still complaining as he thrust in his hand and drew a bean. The Irishman's complaints had added drama to the already dramatic scene, and both Mexicans and Texans watched intently.

He drew a white bean.

The Irishman shook it under the noses of the officers and said, "It started black, but I offered up a prayer to me saint, and St. Patrick he changed it from a black to a white one! Hooray for me, St. Patrick, and old Ireland forever!"[23]

The last three men on the list did not draw as the seventeen black beans were already drawn. The jar was turned upside down and three white beans fell on the ground.

Captain Cameron, who had drawn a white bean, now wept bitterly and begged the officers to execute him and spare his men. His plea was refused. He bade each of the doomed men a tearful farewell. The other men also had wet cheeks, and they "vowed eternal hatred to the authors of this gory outrage so insulting and revolting to humanity,"[24] Some of the Mexican soldiers were also crying openly.

Just before the execution, the unlucky men were tied together with cords, and their eyes were blindfolded. They were set on a log near the wall with their backs to the firing squad. To be shot in the back was a dreadful insult to a soldier. They begged the officer to shoot them in front and at a short distance, saying that they were not afraid to look death in the face. The officer refused.

The Shooting

Nine of the men were executed, then the remaining eight. The other Texans who had drawn the white beans could hear what was happening from their side of the wall. They heard their unlucky comrades being ordered to kneel, could hear the signal taps of the drum, the rattle of the muskets as they were raised, the command to fire, "the sharp burst of the discharge, mingled with the shrill cries of the anguish and heavy groans of the dying."[25]

There was a round of shots, followed by single shots to kill the men who had not died at the first firing. Some of the men were shot six or seven times. The poor quality of the Mexican guns and the poor marksmanship of the Red Caps account for the slow gruesomeness of the execution.

Henry Whaling, cursing his executioners, is said to have been shot fifteen times and in his agony continued shouting defiant profanity. Huerta, perhaps from pity, perhaps from exasperation, placed his pistol to Whaling's temple and fired.[26]

Alfred Thurmond witnessed the execution. As translator, he had earlier been forced to tell his comrades of their impending decimation. We can only imagine what his feelings must have been on being compelled to also view their executions.

Reprieve Comes Late

Back in Mexico City, the Ministers of England, France, and the United States had continued to press Santa Anna to retract his order for the decimation. At last he agreed, and word was sent to Saltillo to spare the men.

It arrived one day late.[27, 28]

CHAPTER 29

Survivors March On

After the Shooting

The bodies were left where they fell. The next morning, guards discovered that one of the bodies was missing. James L. Shepherd, only seventeen years old, had survived and escaped. He was wounded in the cheek and arm, and had fallen in such a way that he was sheltered by the bodies of the dead men. He crawled away during the night and was taken in and cared for by a kind hearted Mexican woman.[1]

Four days later near Saltillo, he was recognized and recaptured. In spite of Santa Anna's late order not to kill the men, he was taken beyond the town and shot by order of Juan Jose Sanchez, Governor of the state of Coahuila.

On the morning after the black bean execution, the prisoners, chained in pairs, set out on their long march to Mexico City. They passed by where the victims still lay, "their rigid countenances pallid and distorted with agony."[2]

Bigfoot on the Long March

The shackles on Bigfoot Wallace were too small and cut deep into his flesh. He was pulling a sick companion, and the effort made his wounds worse. His arms became so swollen and black, he was afraid gangrene had set in.

In San Luis Potosí, the wife of the Governor came to look at the prisoners and noticed Wallace's condition. She ordered that his chains be taken off. The officer in command refused, saying that only the Governor had the authority to give such an order. The lady answered that she was the Governor's wife and repeated her order. She must have had a strong personal bearing because this time the commander sent for a blacksmith.

She saw the suffering of the other prisoners and asked the commander if he was afraid of them without their chains.

He said forcefully that he was not.

The Governor's wife had trapped the commander in his own bravado. She ordered that the chains be cut off all the prisoners. She called for brandy, the best antiseptic available, and bathed the men's infected arms herself. Asa Hill was one of the men she cared for. Bigfoot Wallace told her she ought to be President of Mexico.[3]

Without his chains, Bigfoot could take advantage of his long arms. People commonly carried baskets of bread and other food on their heads. As the prisoners were marched through the towns, Wallace could reach down and help himself to some much needed food. He could also use his long arms to lift tamales and cakes from vendors' stands.[4]

The Texans were such a ghastly, tattered crew that the people along the way were shocked to see them. Their sunken eyes looked "frenzied and ferocious." They seemed like "hideous corpses newly risen from their graves."[5] Bigfoot said he had become such a beauty, his old sweetheart would surely have reconsidered turning him down if she could only have seen him.

Bigfoot's long shirts had been specially made for him back in San Antonio. They came below his knees. When he wore his pants out, the Mexicans thought he was a priest. Some of them would call him Padre and run out and give him a little food.[6]

Going South with Talkin' Bill

Some of the Texans were too sick to march and were allowed to ride in ox carts. Five of the men were so sick they were left in an army hospital in San Luis Potosí where they soon died. The others moved on.

As they traveled southward, the Texans' treatment improved. They no longer had to sleep outside. Instead they had the shelter of abandoned buildings and warehouses. The people of the towns, though very poor, gave the Texans food. The exhausted, miserable captives tried to keep their spirits up.

William Moore, known as Talkin' Bill, had a special talent for building his comrades' morale. George Washington Trahern described him vividly. He recalled that Talkin' Bill would stay back at meals and take his part of the food last. Before he ate, he wanted to be sure no one was left out.

Once, the Mexican cavalry were riding behind the Texans, "whipping up"[7] those who fell behind. Talkin' Bill saw that the wounded Trahern was so tired he could barely walk and was about to drop out. He fell in beside Trahern.

"Hullo, Wash," he said. "Grass is mighty short."[8] Then he went on talking. He "never said anything that anybody else ever said in the world; one of them original cusses; you couldn't help but laugh to save your life; he would keep you in good humor. I revived up and walked forty-five miles that day, just from that fellow's talking to me."[9]

CHAPTER 30

Ewen Cameron

On April 24, 1843, one month after the black bean incident, the main group of prisoners who were with Cameron neared an Indian village called Huehuetoca. Once again nature seemed to predict Texan fate. A storm blew in, fierce as the one that heralded the drawing of the black beans.

A rider galloped from the capital in the middle of the night. Ewen Cameron and the translator, Alfred Thurmond, were awakened. Thurmond was forced to give a terrible message to his leader and friend: Cameron was to be shot at dawn.

Cameron was closely guarded so he couldn't communicate with his men. At dawn the other Texans were marched on their way. Only Cameron and Thurmond were kept be-

---

Ewen Cameron—the Bruce of the West

Born in Scotland and named for the Scottish hero, Sir Ewen Cameron, he lived up to his warrior name. He arrived in Texas during its revolution and served in the Texas army from April through December 1836. His military service was paid for with warrants for 1,920 acres of land which his heirs later claimed in San Patricio County. After the revolution, he defended the Texas frontier with followers known as "Cameron's Cowboys." He was known as a "bold and chivalrous leader" and as "the Bruce of the West." He was a man of little education but great ability, a natural leader. He seems to have been the most beloved man on the Mier expedition. (Cutrer, *Handbook of Texas Online*)

hind. Thurmond had to witness another execution. The Mexican soldiers took Cameron behind the building and made him stand in front of a stone wall. They tied his hands behind him, and started to bandage his eyes. Cameron resisted, saying that for the liberty of Texas he could look death in the face without winking. The soldiers honored his request as that of an officer.

They raised their muskets.

Cameron shouted, "Fire!"

He gave the order that ended his own life. He was thirty-six years old.

CHAPTER 31

John C. C. Hill

John C. C. in Matamoros

John C. C., back in Matamoros, had no idea what had happened to the other Texans. The last time he saw his father, Asa was leaving on the horse John C. C. had requested and General Ampudia had provided for him. At that time, his brother Jeffrey was still in Mier, under the care of General Ampudia's physician, waiting for his wound to heal. John C. C. hadn't heard from his father, his brother, or his mother. He longed to hear from his family. He studied hard to keep from worrying. He had to learn the subjects and also had to learn a new language and a new way of living. However, John C. C. was living a pleasant life with the Ampudia family, and he had reason to believe that his father and brother were being well cared for. He had no idea what was happening to them or to the other fire eaters, but General Ampudia's kind treatment of them gave John C. C. every reason to assume they were all being treated well.

General Ampudia had first been charmed by John C. C.'s courage and later by his intelligence. He always referred to him as his son, and mentioned John C. C. several times in his letters to President General Santa Anna. His glowing praise aroused Santa Anna's interest.

John C. C. had been studying in Matamoros only a few weeks when a letter came from Santa Anna. It said, "I request that the young Texan, Juan Christobal Colon Gil, be sent to me under safe guard by way of Tampico and Rio del Monte to Mexico City."[1]

John C. C. was shocked and confused. Was he to be punished because he had shot so many artillerymen at Mier?

General Ampudia, still in acute grief for his son who died in the Battle of Mier, was heartbroken to also lose the winning youth he had expected to rear and educate. But he had no choice; Santa Anna's word was law.

General Ampudia must have been concerned about the boy's safety on the long journey. The difficult trail John C. C. had traveled from San Antonio to Mier was less than half the distance he would have to go to reach Mexico City. The trip could be expected to take at least a month. It would be arduous and dangerous. He would have to cross rugged mountains. He might fall into the hands of some of the many robbers who preyed on travelers.

General Ampudia saw to it that the boy had reliable escorts—a captain, a lieutenant, and several soldiers. He also gave him a beautiful horse and saddle for the long trip. The contrast between the journey before John C. C. and the same journey being made by the other fire eaters could hardly be more dramatic. They were walking in chains. He was going as the protégé of a general to become the protégé of an absolute dictator. He was fourteen and bewildered.

John C. C. in Mexico City

John C. C. arrived in Mexico City in March of 1843. He expected to be taken immediately into the fearful presence of Santa Anna—the man Texans most hated—the Butcher of the Alamo—the man responsible for the massacre at Goliad—

and, though John C.C. didn't yet know it, the man responsible for the death lottery of the black beans.

As it turned out, Santa Anna was sick and could not see him, so John C. C. had weeks to dread the meeting. However, he stayed at one of the most splendid homes in Mexico City, the palace of the Archbishop.

Archbishop Posada received John C. C. kindly. When he told his story, the Archbishop realized that the boy was suffering terrible anxiety about his father, brother, and friends. Knowing the healing power of nature, the archbishop took him into one of the sheltered patio gardens and reassured him, saying that everything was in God's hands. John C. C. was comforted by the Archbishop's kindness and by the gentle beauty of the garden.

At last, the dreaded summons came. An orderly was sent to escort John C. C. across the square to the magnificent Presidential Palace. It covered ten acres. It was not only Santa Anna's home, it also contained the offices of public servants and the courts of justice. John C. C. was ushered into the awful presence of Santa Anna, the Napoleon of the West. His "Serene Highness" sat on a dais. Draperies of red and gold hung on both sides of the ruler's chair. Portraits of Mexico's great men lined the walls.

John C. C. walked to the edge of the dais. Santa Anna extended his hand and invited John C. C. to come nearer.

"Well, my young friend," he said, "I am glad to meet you for I have heard a great deal about you. They tell me that you killed several of my Mexicans at Mier."[2]

John C. C. answered that he did not know how many he had killed but that he had fired fifteen or twenty times. Then he asked Santa Anna to release him.

Santa Anna said, "Very well, I will release you and what is more, I will adopt you as my son and educate and provide for you."[3]

John C. C. told Santa Anna that he already had loving and devoted parents. Santa Anna introduced John C. C. to General Jose Marie Tornel, Minister of War and former Minister to the United States. The strikingly handsome Tornel was one of the most learned and scholarly men of his day.

John C. C. couldn't possibly have realized just how important this occasion was. Busy and powerful men were discussing his future welfare. Santa Anna proposed to send John C. C. to Chapultepec Military Academy to become an officer in the army.

John C. C. admitted that he would like to attend one of the fine schools in Mexico, but said that he could not agree to anything without the consent of his father. He also said he could not go to a Mexican military school because there might be a war with Texas. In that case, he said, "I would go home and serve in the ranks. I should never fight my own country."[4]

Santa Anna—the Napoleon of the West

President General Santa Anna was forty-four years old — a handsome man with a commanding presence. He had a harsh voice but could move and sway men through powerful speeches. He was about five feet ten inches tall, well proportioned with an athletic build. His bearing was military in spite of his having lost a leg. His large dark eyes were both expressive and intelligent. He had a complex personality. He readily endured hardship but loved luxury and collected art and antiquities. Fanny Calderon, writer and wife of the first Spanish ambassador to the republic of Mexico, visited him at his estate, Magna de Clavo. She found him gentlemanly, handsome, rather melancholy looking, and quite interesting. He often referred to himself as "The Napoleon of the West," a name he thought of as befitting a conquerer, since Napoleon's short reign was still fresh in memory.

Rather than feeling annoyed at this reply, Santa Anna was pleased by the boy's courage. General Tornel seemed amused.

General Tornel said, "Your Excellency, I feel sure our young friend would like the *Mineria*." The *Mineria* was one of the finest schools of engineering in the world. Tornel continued, "If you will permit me, I shall be glad to have him come into my family as a third son, and he shall have two nationalities, and not have to fight either."[5]

John C. C. liked the idea of attending the *Mineria* and becoming an engineer. However, he insisted he would have to talk to his father about the offer. He said that he had made a vow to take care of his father and brother and that he was anxious for news about them.

Santa Anna saw how sincerely upset his protégé was. He took one of John C. C.'s hands in his and put his other hand on the boy's head. "I will do all in my power to find out something about them."[6]

Then John C. C. was taken to Santa Anna's private quarters to meet Doña Inés, the first lady of Mexico. She was a gentle, affectionate woman of thirty-two. She had grown up working hard, and in spite of her rank, was simple and unassuming in her manner.

John C. C. was moved from the Bishop's Palace into the Presidential Palace with Santa Anna and Doña Inés. He was given complete liberty, and every care was taken for his comfort. He was made a part of their normal life and often shared afternoon rides with them in the presidential carriage.

A Letter from Home

One day a government courier brought a letter addressed to Juan C. C. Hill de Ampudia. A letter had come to Matamoros from John C. C.'s mother, and General Ampudia had made sure that it was sent to Mexico City promptly. There is no record of what was in the letter; it was probably simple news about the family and farm. The arrival of any letter was a big occasion, however. To receive a letter from Texas was difficult. Not only was the distance long, but there had been no mail service of any kind between Texas and Mexico since Texas became a Republic. Mail went by way of the United States and was unreliable. That John C. C. received the letter shows General Ampudia's kindness and continuing concern.

CHAPTER 32

Maverick in Perote

About four months earlier—on December 22, 1842—Sam Maverick and the other San Antonio captives had reached Perote Castle where they were to be imprisoned. The battle at Mier, supposedly to rescue them, had not even taken place when they were locked away in those grim walls.

Perote was like a small walled town with a moat that enclosed the castle and various other buildings. The enormous compound, built to accommodate two thousand people, was formidable and the area was gloomy. The weather was cold and damp all year long, and the mountain peaks were usually hidden in thick clouds. No one had ever escaped from the Perote prison.

Sam Maverick and his compatriots insisted that the Texans in San Antonio had believed they were defending themselves against a large band of frontier desperados. They pointed out that there were many such bands in the area and insisted that they had no intention of going against the Mexican government.[1]

Maverick Agitates

On January 5, 1843, Maverick was placed in solitary confinement for making complaints on behalf of the prisoners. However, he refused to be silenced, and wrote a letter to the Mexican secretary of state, Jose María Bocanegra, protesting both the captives' detention and their inhumane treatment. "We are chained by the legs with heavy ox chains, coupled like beasts, two and two together and forced at the point of the bayonet side by side with your shameless convicted felons,—robbers and murderers."[2] He also complained about having to do dirty, heavy work without enough food. However, Maverick was careful to emphasize that he was speaking on his own, not as a representative of the other men. This was to prevent others from being punished for the complaints.

Maverick also repeatedly petitioned for release. His cousin, Waddy Thompson, U.S. Minister to Mexico, was working to free him. Maverick knew that he could have his freedom any time he liked if he would only say that he was in favor of the reannexation of Texas to Mexico. Waddy Thompson explained that the Mexicans only wanted to save face with an agreement that recognized Mexican sovereignty, and that Texas would continue to have broad independent powers. Maverick wouldn't say such a thing, even for his freedom.

He wrote, "I cannot persuade myself that such an annexation, on any terms, would be advantageous to Texas, and I therefore cannot say so, for I regard a lie as a crime, and one which I cannot commit even to secure my release; I must, therefore, continue to wear my chains, galling as they are."[3]

On March 16, 1843, Maverick received a letter from his wife. It had taken three months to arrive, and was the only one he received during his captivity. Although Maverick appears to have managed to keep his spirits up, prison did have its effect. Locked up with nothing to see or take his attention, his logical, reasoned approach to life began to be replaced by mystic, poetic thoughts. He recognized this, and his journal on the day he received the letter reads, "Reflections, memories, inferences and dreams have occupied my soul. In spite of my former indifference to dreams they now occupy me much; and are in fact the most interesting events of my life."[4]

Maverick Goes Home

On March 22, 1843, Maverick's journal says that he, Jones, and Judge Hutchinson had their chains taken off and that horses were ready to take them to Mexico City for release.[5] In Mexico City, the three were "first paraded for a quarter of an hour, ragged and dirty, in front of the Palace—then escorted into it."[6] This was done to show the power of the government, which was actually quite weak. It served to degrade the prisoners under the pretense of generosity. It also entertained the masses and served to remind them that the consequences of rebellion were severe. The rest of the San Antonio captives remained imprisoned at Perote.

Ironically Maverick, Jones, and Hutchinson were officially liberated from Perote on March 30, 1843, at almost the same time that Thomas Jefferson Green and William Fisher were being imprisoned there. Maverick, Jones and Hutchinson remained briefly in Mexico City, and Maverick arrived home on May 4, 1843. He was back with his family before most of his would-be rescuers had even reached their final destinations as prisoners.

CHAPTER 33

Green's Group Arrives at Perote

In late March 1843, General Green, General Fisher, and their group reached the Perote prison. They were taken into a big empty room about seventy feet wide and twenty feet long. The only light in the room came through a small opening in the wall and through a small grating in the door. There was no furniture, and the stone floor and walls were cold and damp. Ever since their surrender at Mier, the officers and their entourage had had privileged treatment, but now the pleasant times were over.

Green and Fisher had no idea what had happened to the other men from the Mier expedition. Their last contact with them was outside Salado when they cheered for their comrades' escape.

On their first morning in Perote, Green, and Fisher met the very men they had gone on the Mier expedition to free — all the men General Woll had captured in San Antonio, except Maverick, Jones, and Hutchinson, who had just been freed. The San Antonio captives had arrived the very day the battle at Mier was fought. They had been in Perote about four months.

Life in Perote Prison

The prisoners in Perote were required to work. Those who had skills, such as carpentry, were able to work using

Green's Group Arrives at Perote 151

their skills. Others were given various jobs maintaining the castle and grounds. Both General Green and General Fisher refused to work, saying that they were officers and were therefore exempt.

In the early 1800s, the class a person was born into was even more important than his nationality. Although a person could rise from humble origins in the Republic of Texas and in the United States, class consciousness remained an important factor in the society. In Mexico, where no pretense of equality existed, the class system was a very strong factor indeed.

General Green and General Fisher continued to use this class consciousness to their advantage. Although they were often threatened, they never had to work like the men of lesser rank. Green and Fisher also had the advantage of money. They had obtained gifts and loans on the way to Perote so were not in pressing need as most of their comrades were.

The Texan's values had not changed with imprisonment. It was a matter of pride to them never to show a loss of spirit. When the guards put chains on them, the Texans thanked them as if the guards were doing them a big favor. They called the chains their jewelry. When they were being starved, some of the Texans sang loudly to show their indifference to suffering.[1]

Many used their time creatively. When they could get paper, some drew pictures of Perote and their surroundings. A spoon and two pipes which Norman Woods made from small pieces of wood are on display at the Alamo. Some of the men were skilled carpenters and managed to make fiddles. A man named Journeay made one using an old razor blade, a file, and a few pieces of broken glass. He put tiny arrow-shaped inlaid work on the bridge and made the tail piece from soup bones, which he carved. The bow was made from a piece of wood left over from Santa Anna's chair of state.[2]

When the fiddlers in the group played, the other Texans sometimes danced, shaking their legs, rattling their chains,

and stepping lively on their sore, swollen feet. McCutchan wrote, "These amusements and laughs are not of the heart. We go to extremes in gaiety to prevent despondency."[3]

The Texans could tolerate being chained and having to sleep on the cold stone floor, but they couldn't bear to take off their hats when the Governor passed. They preferred to take a beating. "Inhale a small quantity of the air of Liberty for me. I have almost forgotten the smell of it," one prisoner wrote to a friend.[4]

In spite of the Texans' devoting themselves full time to annoying their guards, friendly relationships developed. Some were so friendly that they caused problems. Once a fight broke out in the laundry room because a Mexican lieutenant caught Isaac Allen in a compromising situation with his wife. Allen defended her virtue and his honor vigorously, insisting all the while that he had only given the lady an innocent kiss to thank her for washing his shirt.[5]

CHAPTER 34

The Fire Eaters Arrive in Mexico City

A gateman at the Presidential Palace told John C. C. Hill that the Texans would arrive soon. He watched for them eagerly. One day he heard a noise. Citizens were exclaiming about four ragged, barefoot boys being escorted down the street by Mexican soldiers. John C. C. saw that they were his friends, fire eaters Orlando Phelps, Gilbert Brush, Harvey Sellers, and Billy Reese. He called out to them and stopped the soldiers.

What he saw was startling. John C. C., himself well fed, well dressed, and living in luxury, saw that Billy Reese was sick and all the fire eaters were hungry and exhausted. He determined to help them. Yet, John C. C.'s friends had something he did not—information. He knew nothing of what had happened since he had been taken up by General Ampudia after the battle of Mier. They told John C. C. about the revolt at Hacienda de Salado, about the drawing of the black beans, that his father had drawn a white bean, and that Captain Cameron had been executed. They also told him that they believed his father was still alive and would soon reach the capital.[1]

John C. C. asked Santa Anna to free the fire eaters. This was a brave move. Although John C. C.'s life was comfortable, it was precarious. The changeable Santa Anna was

154

known for his dramatic shifts of mood. He could not be lightly opposed. He had taken John C. C. up on a whim and could discard him as quickly.

Santa Anna did not agree to free the fire eaters, but he noticed that one was named Orlando Phelps. Dr. James A. E. Phelps had once saved his life. When Santa Anna was himself in captivity after the Battle of San Jacinto, and was himself not being well treated, he fell into such despair over his defeat that he tried to kill himself by taking an overdose of laudanum. Dr. Phelps pumped the narcotic out of his stomach and cared for him in his own home. Santa Anna was grateful.

Santa Anna had Orlando brought to him. He asked the boy if he were related to Dr. Phelps of Orozimbo, and Orlando answered that Dr. Phelps was his father. Santa Anna immediately ordered Orlando's release, had new clothes bought for him, and let him share John C. C.'s room in the palace.

In the meantime, Billy Reese had become so sick he was taken to the Hospital de Jesus Nazarene. John C. C. and Orlando visited him there before Orlando left for home. Orlando was sent back to Texas at Santa Anna's personal expense and was provided with money for whatever he might want on the journey. He left by stagecoach for Veracruz where he caught a schooner about May 5 and reached New Orleans on May 22, 1843.

Billy Reese Meets Santa Anna

John C. C. continued trying to help his friends. He asked Waddy Thompson, U.S. Minister to Mexico and Maverick's cousin, to talk to Santa Anna about freeing the other fire eaters. Thompson constantly asked for the release of the Mier men, but there was a limit to how many individual prisoners he could ask to be released. However, he took a fancy to Billy Reese and requested that Santa Anna grant him an audience. General Ampudia also had taken a special interest in Billy and had already contacted Santa Anna, asking that Billy be released.

When Billy was well enough, Waddy Thompson, along with John C. C., took him to see the President. John C. C. boldly asked for Billy's freedom. But Billy said he did not want to be sent home. He said he wanted to go to the Perote prison to take the place of his brother, Captain Charles Reese. He said Charles was engaged to be married and that he would be of more use to their parents than Billy himself would.

Santa Anna told Billy that he had barely recovered from a long illness and was in no condition to endure the Perote prison. He must go home.

Billy had to accept this decision. But in spite of his helpless condition and his physical weakness, Billy continued to press his small advantage, just as the half-dead Cameron had done when recaptured in the desert mountains. Perhaps this soldierly courage was what had captured the attention of General Ampudia and of Waddy Thompson and attracted them to Billy.

He asked permission to visit Perote and see his brother.

Santa Anna agreed.

Santa Anna told Waddy Thompson that it was foolish to ever liberate any Texan because Texans just came back to fight again. Billy spoke up and said that indeed, he would fight again.[2] But Santa Anna was patient with the brash fire eater, and ordered that he be sent home.

John C. C. and Billy Visit Perote

Before he left, Billy was allowed to visit his brother in Perote prison, 160 miles away. John C. C. went with him. John C. C. and Billy passed the guard house outside Perote, and then a bridge was lowered for them over the moat. The horses hooves clattered as the boys rode over the bridge, and up to the plaza that was surrounded by the Texans' prison rooms. The spirited Texans made the reunion a happy one and gave Billy a farewell party. They provided a feast and entertainment.

"Sailing Master Lyons browned coffee beans and ground

them on a flat stone. Dan Henrie sang 'Long, Long Ago' and 'The Soldier's Tear' as he waved a fan to encourage their small fire. General Fisher hashed beef while Lieutenant Clark peeled potatoes and mangled peppers. Charlie Reese stood over the fire, stirring the *burra* milk that had been mixed with water, coffee, eggs and sugar . . . General Green, after frequent tastings, pronounced his approval and all hands agreed."[3]

William Trimble, "with a flashing dare-devil expression in his eye"[4] rolled his eyes back in their sockets, twisted his head "clean round: on his shoulders and gave a whoop that beat the best of owls."[5] The Mexican captain who had looked in to see what all the commotion was about, pointed his finger at Trimble and said, "*Tecolote!*" This is the Spanish for *owl*, and Tecolote was Trimble's name from then on.

The party ended with the imprisoned Texans toasting Billy Reese with mescal. They sent him off with bundles of letters.

Fire eaters Gilbert Brush and Harvey Sellers had a harder lot. They were treated as ordinary prisoners. John C. C. was not able to help them.

Perote Castle

Perote Castle still stands. It is located less than a mile from the village of Perote in the state of Veracruz. It is situated in a narrow valley 7,000 feet above sea level. The surrounding mountains are usually hidden by clouds, and the castle is cold all year. Freezing rains are common even in summer. Originally the Castle of San Carlos, it was built by Spain in the 1770s to make a trade route safe and to hold treasure. Comfort was not a consideration. It is a stone fortress surrounded by a moat. The compound covers about twenty-six acres. The moat is 150 feet wide and the walls measure sixty feet from the bottom of the moat to the top. Perote was equipped to hold two thousand people. The prisoners held there were largely political and military captives, rather than criminals. The castle served as retirement home for General Don Guadalupe Victoria, former President of Mexico, and was often used by Santa Anna and Doña Ines when they traveled from Mexico City to their estate at Jalapa. The castle grounds were like a small town, with houses, stables, and workshops surrounding a concrete plaza where there was usually a bustle of activity. (Conner, np; Haynes, 136-137)

CHAPTER 35

Asa Hill's Decision

Asa Arrives in Mexico City

Some time after the arrival of the fire eaters, the main group of Texan prisoners arrived. It was just two days after the execution of Ewen Cameron. These men who had been with him were secured in the convent at Santiago Tlaltelolco, two miles from the northern entrance gate to Mexico City.[1] They had marched 800 miles since they surrendered at Mier—not including their miles of wandering after the escape from Haciendo del Salado.

The fire eaters had told John C. C. these men would soon arrive, and he watched for them eagerly. On April 26, 1843, he saw a line of men lurching toward the plaza. He ran toward them, elbowing through the crowd, and found that they were Texan prisoners. A blacksmith was just fastening chains to their ankles. One of the prisoners was bearded, dirty, frail Asa Hill.

John C. C. demanded that his father not be bound. Then he ran to the Presidential Palace and found Santa Anna. He told him that his father had arrived walking, that he looked like a ghost, and that he was being chained.

Santa Anna ordered Asa's chains removed and had him sent to the Hospital de Jesus Nazarene. He invited Asa to the palace for a talk about John C. C.'s future as soon as he was well enough. Doña Inés had her own cook prepare soup for Asa, and John C. C. visited him every day, always laden with flowers and treats.

When Asa recovered, he was outfitted in new clothes and was received at the Presidential Palace. Santa Anna explained that he admired John C. C. and wanted to keep him in Mexico where he would provide him with the best possible education.

Asa could readily see that these were exceptional advantages for a Texas farm boy. He appreciated the opportunity being offered. There were hardly any schools in Texas at that time, certainly no universities, whereas the *Mineria* was a university of international reputation. Although Asa recognized the generosity of Santa Anna's offer and saw its advantages, he had some requests. He did not want John C. C. to become a Mexican citizen, did not want him to change his Methodist religion, and wanted him to keep in close contact with his family. He also emphasized that he wanted John C. C. to be free to make his own choices.

Asa's own adoption of Joseph Mendes may have helped him have more understanding of the Mexicans than many Texans did. Indeed, some of the Texans were horrified at John C. C.'s adoption and thought that Asa was a foolish old man who sold his son for his freedom. The truth is that Asa showed extraordinary wisdom, not only in recognizing the importance of the education and the contacts that were being offered to John C. C., but also in his understanding of his son's exceptional skill in getting along with people. Most boys could not have managed his difficult situation. Asa also must have known that John C. C. would not lose touch with his family as many boys in his place would have done. Perhaps he also hoped for what indeed came to pass—John C. C. would serve both countries well.

Santa Anna readily agreed to Asa's conditions and said that he would do everything in his power to equip John C. C. for a happy and useful life. He added that he would arrange for Asa's transportation home and would do the same for Jeffrey when he arrived.

John C. C. had indeed fulfilled his vow to take care of his father and brother.

Another Family for John C. C.

John C. C. moved into the Tornel home and began studies at the *Mineria*. He had already formed a warm friendship with General Tornel's sons, Augustine and Manuel. The Tornels, like Santa Anna and General Ampudia, considered John C. C. their son. Once more John C. C. threw himself into his studies, this time with the goal of becoming an engineer.

CHAPTER 36

The Prisoners at Molina Del Rey

The other newly arrived prisoners, less fortunate than Asa Hill, were told that they were going to be put to work. They were given convict clothes made of white flannel with red and green vertical stripes. The Texans complained to the soldiers about the bright, clownish prison clothes, but they joked among themselves. It was actually a relief to have clean clothes of any kind.

The men, including fire eaters Gilbert Brush and Harvey Sellers, were marched to the outskirts of Mexico City to a pleasant village called Tacubaya. It was on the slope of the Sierra de las Cruces mountains. The Texans were to build a road from Santa Anna's summer home in Tacubaya into Mexico City. They were housed in a complicated range of low stone buildings with a flour mill at one end and a foundry at the other end. It was called Molina del Rey. The prisoners could walk about the grounds when they were not working. The Texans were each given the luxury of a straw mat, but no blanket. Some of the Texans had blankets of their own that they had carried on the long road.

They were put in the charge of an idealistic young captain. He spoke to them very courteously and promised that he would do everything to make their task an easy one. He explained the grading of the road, its width, and the method of construction. He believed in cooperation and even assigned Texans as overseers.

The Texans didn't give the young officer any cooperation. They managed to do almost no work at all. One of the diarists bragged that they got less done in two months than a pair of Irishmen could get done in a week.

Naturally, the kind young captain was soon replaced. The Texan overseers were replaced with Mexican convicts and the new captain, saying that he would tolerate no more laziness, ordered two men to be taken out of line and clubbed.[1] The other Texans raised their shovels and picks and started after the guards. Surprisingly, the officer ordered that the two men be released.

The food was so foul that even the half-starved Texans often could not eat it. Several times, however, they were surprised with a good meal prepared and sent to them by the ladies of the village. President Santa Anna and Doña Inés often took John C. C. with them when they visited their villa in Tacubaya. He could then go and visit with the prisoners. John C. C. was upset to see his friends' treatment, but he was relieved that his father was spared their hardships. He spoke to Santa Anna again, asking for better conditions. Doña Inés joined her voice to John C. C.'s and even asked for the Texans' release, but Santa Anna was not persuaded.[2]

Even though punishment was severe, the Texans managed to delay the building of the road. They cut slits in the sacks they were given to carry rocks in so that most of them fell out. They walked slowly and stumbled. They broke and hid their tools.

The guards hitched the strongest prisoners to wagons and had them pull loads of rocks. Of course, Bigfoot Wallace was hitched to a wagon as he was one of the very strongest men. One day he grabbed a cart, neighed like a horse, and galloped down the hill. Mexican guards shouted at him, but he wouldn't stop. He hurtled along as fast as he could go. When he reached a curve, he jumped out of the way and let the wagon go rushing along on its own. The wagon wrecked. Bigfoot was sure he would be punished, but instead the guards laughed.

Some of the Texans pretended to be sick, thinking they would be able to rest. Instead, their treatment was to be stripped naked, kept in bed, and fed a little cornmeal gruel and a lot of castor oil. Their health improved wonderfully.

The Texans said later that they could have finished the one hundred yards of road in ten days, but they had managed to string the work out for two full months.[3] The Mexicans finally set up a reward system, which was a more successful approach. Texans were willing to work for food or to have their chains removed.

CHAPTER 37

Jeffrey Hill

John Day Morgan and nine of the wounded who had been left in Matamoros had started toward Mexico City in early March. They took the road to Tampico.

On March 5, five more of the wounded started toward Mexico City following the same route. The group included Jeffrey Hill and J. D. McCutchan. These men were much weakened by their wounds, and suffered on the road. They were fed only once a day even though they made long marches every day. On April 23, after a forty-three day march, they reached Tampico, worn out and nearly naked. In Tampico they were better treated. Jeffrey Hill and J. D. McCutchan were allowed to stroll around the town, followed by two soldiers who walked a respectable distance behind them so they could enjoy a sense of privacy. On their walk they met a black man, evidently a former slave, who was moved by their situation. He chatted with them and expressed his sympathy. This is another instance of the remarkable feelings escaped slaves showed, even though the Texans were clearly members of the slave-holding culture.

Franklin E. Chase, United States Consul, and some U.S merchants were also saddened at the Texans' situation. They gave them clothes and money.

When the Texans continued toward Mexico City, they were in the hands of Lieutenant Francisco Padrajo and seven sergeants. Lieutenant Padrajo and one of the sergeants had been prisoners in Texas. Amazingly, this seemed to establish a bond. They allowed the Texans to ride horses with no restraint after they merely promised not to escape. They were even allowed to visit a theater and to socialize with various English speaking people along the way. Jeffrey Hill and the others in this group kept their promise and did not try to escape.

The day before they reached Mexico City, Lieutenant Padrajo told the Texans, "It will be best for you now to dismount; let me send the horses back and you walk into the city, all of you. For were you to ride into the presence of the Commanding General, he would say to you—'You are not fatigued, therefore go immediately to work,' and you would be put in chains and made to work tomorrow. But if you walk in, he will think you very much fatigued with the journey and will give you a few days rest."[1] Of course, the men agreed. They were allowed to rest in Mexico City for five days. They were then taken to Molina del Rey and reunited with the Texans there.

Jeffrey Hill Goes Home

Jeffrey Hill was sent to the hospital and then, like his father, was freed, just as Santa Anna had promised. On his way to Veracruz to catch a ship home, Jeffrey stopped by Perote to see his friends and carry letters for them. In Veracruz, the local officials arrested Jeffrey and put him in prison. This must have been a heart-stopping event for him. He was without help from Texas and knew no one in Veracruz. But the U.S. Consul spoke for him and he was again liberated. He managed to catch a ship and arrived safely home.[2] It had been a long and painful trail. He was wounded at Mier, was sick throughout his imprisonment, and seems to have borne his misfortune patiently.

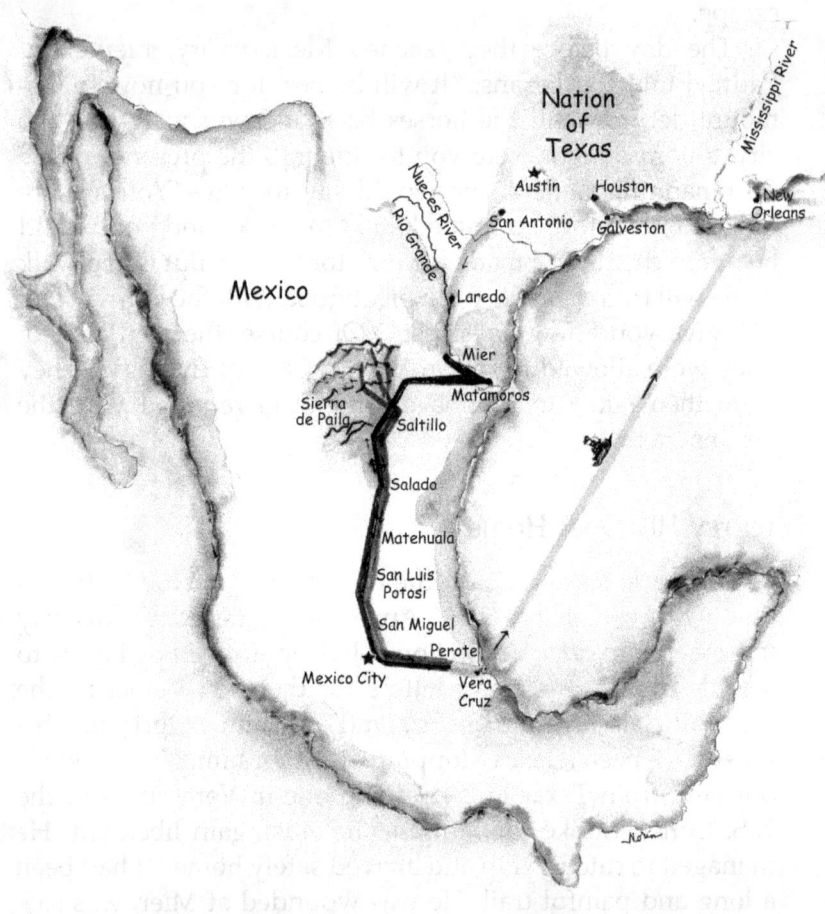

Captive Texans suffered greatly on the long march from Mier to Perote, but freed Texans sailed quickly from Veracruz to New Orleans.

CHAPTER 38

Letters Home

The Perote prisoners wrote long letters home even though they knew that the letters might never reach their destination. The trip from Mexico to the U.S. and then to the Republic of Texas was long and uncertain, but the letters carried by friends, like the ones carried by Jeffrey Hill and Asa Hill always reached their destinations. Asa had carried a letter from Norman Woods to his wife, Jane. In it, Norman says, "never heard of Gonzalvoes escape until January you have no idea the satisfaction it gave me to think that he had made his escape and that I still had a Brother that would take care of you & our little family."[1]

In their letters, some of the Texans painted a rosy pictures of their lives in order not to worry their families. Norman Woods wrote cheerful and optimistic letters to his wife, Jane. "We have plenty to eat, good clothes to wear, coffee twice a day, meat once, good flour bread. I am coopering and make bout one well bucket a week."[2]

When he wrote his brother, Gonzalvo, he was more honest. He said that his shattered hip had left him crippled. It had not healed as it should, and he suffered constant pain. He worried about his family and asked his brother to see that his children were schooled. "Being satisfied that you will pay my family every possible attention relieves my mind in no inconsiderable degree."[3]

It is interesting to remember that Gonzalvo himself was not well schooled, and it is a tribute to him and to the quality of the brothers' relationship that Norman could so confidently depend on him to educate the children, not just put them to work as was so often done in that day.

This letter to Gonzalvo carried a postscript by E. Y. Keene. It is written in Norman's handwriting. Apparently Keene was illiterate. The postscript reads:

> I fool the Mexicans out of many a days work . . . raise good crops as I expect to retuen . . . verry poor and will have to live on my friends until I fatten up. I want you to lay an embargo on all the girls in that vacinity and keep them from marrying off so fast . . . I deputize you in my name to go and see all the girls in pullet prairie and give them one good kiss each in my name, but do not tell us of any more weddings or I shall Run entirely crazy as you will perceive by reading this that my head is partly cracked already.[4]

When Jeffrey Hill and his companions arrived at Molina del Rey and reunited with the prisoners there, J. D. McCutchan wrote in his diary:

> Sweet is the meeting of fellow soldiers, suffering in the same sacred cause. . . . We were one and the same people, enduring hardships in the same glorious cause of liberty; we had fought and suffered for the same ungrateful country, . . . The grip of the hand of a fellow soldier in the same cause, and a fellow sufferer under the same cruelties, is far more preferable, and gives more real joy, than . . . even the welcome embrace of friends in prosperity. *We were one and the same family.*[5]

CHAPTER 39

Escapes from Molina del Rey

The Texans believed they would be released soon because important officials, such as U.S. Minister to Mexico, Waddy Thompson, were working for their freedom. Also, they learned that a British warship had arrived at Veracruz with official letters from the Republic of Texas and that commissioners were on the way to make a deal with Mexico. So for two months they made no attempt to escape.

At the end of two months, the guards had relaxed and developed friendly relationships with their prisoners. They sometimes even took the Texans into town to visit taverns with them. On July 29, 1843, a prisoner named Willis Copeland took advantage of the situation and left. It was twenty-four hours before the guards noticed that he was missing. He managed to make it almost to Matamoros but was recaptured at the Rio Grande within sight of freedom.

Six other Texans also escaped from Molina del Rey at various times. The guards were anxious to avoid blame, so they reported that the Texans had died.

Sam Walker Escapes

Sam Walker felt sure all the Texans would be chained again as a result of Copeland's escape. He had been planning his own escape, but now he needed to hurry. Walker, James C. Wilson, and D. H. Gattis had managed to hide some torn strips of blanket at a far corner of the wooded grounds, near the broad wall that surrounded the old mill. They were able to steal five biscuits as provisions. The evening after Copeland's escape, and before his absence had been discovered, they made their own break for freedom.[1] Just before sunset, they casually strolled by the guards, climbed the wall and used their torn strips of blanket to let themselves down. The night was not a dark one, but the three Texans made it across the wall without alerting the guards.

When their guard at Molina del Rey discovered that three of his prisoners had run away, he slammed the butt of his gun on the floor. He was afraid to report the escape; the officers didn't find out until the next morning; and the Texans had a good head start.

Walker, Wilson, and Gattis made it into Mexico City, where they had to dodge the guards stationed all around town. They swam across a moat to the village of Guadalupe. When morning came on July 31, they had traveled about eighteen miles beyond Mexico City and had eaten all of the biscuits. The three men were exhausted.

They found a comfortable spot where they could lie hidden in some bushes, and each man took a turn on watch while the other two slept. Then they discovered to their dismay that their comfortable hideaway was a meeting place for a group of local shepherd boys. They managed to avoid being discovered, and at twilight they moved on. They were stopped by two maguey farmers, but Walker gave them a dollar, and the farmers let them go.

The next day, they weren't so lucky. Four men found them and turned them in to the village alcalde. He locked them in jail for the night, but didn't bother to post a guard at their door. Using almost the last of their strength, the three Texans managed to pry the door off its hinges and were on their way again. They stayed away from roads and dodged goat herders on the hillsides.

Later they were captured by some *rancheros*. They told the *rancheros* that they were mine workers. Walker happened to have a piece of paper with the words to an old song on it. He showed it to the *rancheros*. They demanded that he translate it. Walker told them that he wasn't good at translating, but he would try. He thought fast and made up a passport. The *rancheros* let the three Texans go. That was good luck, but by now they hadn't eaten anything for five days.

At last when they reached Real del Monte, English residents gave them food, clothes, and even passports. Wilson was so sick he had to stay there to recover, but Walker and Gattis went on and arrived in Tampico on August 12, 1843. They found jobs on a U.S. ship as working seamen and thus made it home. Later, Wilson also got home via Tampico.[2]

John Day Morgan Escapes

A Mexican soldier suspected that John Day Morgan was one of the men who had been captured at Santa Fe. Those captives had been freed after promising, on pain of death, never to take up arms against Mexico again. The soldier questioned him closely. Morgan tried to hide the truth, but he knew the Mexican had not believed him. Morgan was almost sure to be shot, so he decided to risk making an escape. He planned it carefully and chose three friends to go with him. They had to steal a rope and hide it so that they could cross the wall. Then they would make their way to a nearby British paper mill.

One of Morgan's chosen companions was William Thompson. For some time, Thompson had pretended to be crippled. By doing so, he got to ride all the way to Mexico City. He had kept his feet and legs wrapped in bloody rags, and when he walked he limped terribly and made wry faces. He would often grimace and fall when put on his feet. Bigfoot Wallace said that he himself would rather walk or work than make all the faces and contortions that Thompson did.[3] However, Thompson's deceit did more than let him ride. It meant that no one bothered to watch him. Perhaps it was the wily Thompson who, unwatched, was able to steal the rope to cross the wall.

On August 25, 1843, John Day Morgan, Robert Michael Crawford, John Fitzgerald, and Thompson climbed on each other's shoulders to get on top of the wall around Molina del Rey. They used the rope to haul the last man up and to lower themselves down on the other side. The guards were much surprised that *el pobre cojo*, the poor cripple, was gone.[4]

As John Day Morgan had planned, they were able to make their way to the paper mill. The Englishmen there were willing to take the risk of concealing the escaped prisoners. They even began considering ways to help the Texans get out of the country. They hid them for about three weeks. When the excitement of the escape had died down, the Texans' new friends whisked them to the home of the English minister. There, they were feasted for two days. They gathered strength and courage for the dangerous trip home. The minister gave each of them $20 and had them taken outside Mexico City well hidden in a closed carriage.

The Texans then, as they had been directed, walked to an English silver mine where they were given positions as guards for a shipment of silver going to Veracruz. One of their stops was at the Perote prison.

As John Day Morgan was walking with one of the guards, he was startled to hear the guard say, "We have a good many Texans confined here!"

The guard spoke for some time about the Texans and finished his story by saying, "Poor fellows! They fought manfully at Mier, and after all had to be brought here and put to work!"

Morgan was suspicious of the guard's sincerity, so he answered, "That is mild punishment. They ought to be taken out and shot!"[5]

After they arrived at Veracruz with the silver, John Day Morgan and his comrades caught a ship for New Orleans and made it home.

Back in Mexico, the Texans still at Molina del Rey finished

Santa Anna's road and were marched to Perote Castle. It was the first week in September 1843, almost a year since the volunteers had originally gathered. Now they would learn how well off they had been at Molina del Rey.

CHAPTER 40

Escape from Perote

Earlier, in June 1843, after being in Perote Castle three months, General Thomas Jefferson Green decided that the time was ripe for an escape. He invited General William Fisher and Captain Charles Reese to join him.

General Fisher decided he would not try to escape. Many thought the Texans were in prison because he had ordered the surrender at Mier. He did not think it would be right to leave his men now. However, Captain Charles Reese, who had argued against the break at Salado, wanted to make the attempt. His younger brother, fire eater Billy Reese, was safe at home, and Captain Charles Reese was now willing to take the risk.

The Texans had many obstacles to overcome. No one had ever escaped from Perote. If they did manage to get out of Perote, they knew nothing about the countryside there. They were easy to identify, and if they were caught, they would surely be shot.

General Thomas Jefferson Green, whose high opinion of himself was often well deserved, was able once again to use circumstances to their advantage. A wagon went into the village near Perote Castle every day to pick up mail and supplies. Sometimes Texan prisoners went along to carry the supplies or to do other tasks. Green took advantage of this opportunity, no doubt using his powers of persuasion and his rank. At the post office, he managed, although closely watched, to make contact with a man who happened to be there. Then his luck, and his cash, served him well. The man had a map of the area. Green persuaded him to sell it. Then a Texan with the unlikely name of Ludovic Colquhoun, who was skilled in drawing, made copies of the map. Now the Texans had a better chance of getting away once they got out. All that remained was to do what had never been done before — escape from the Perote prison.

Green and Reese prepared to go down the wall outside their high prison cells. They bribed guards and bought rope, but they were not alone in thinking that the time was right for escape. Even though Perote was made of stone and their cell was on an upper level, some of the prisoners who had been captured in San Antonio had begun carving a tunnel through the stone floor and through the walls of their high cell. The tunnelers asked Green and Reese to delay their escape. They were afraid of what fierce action the authorities might take after the loss of two Texan officers, and they didn't want anything to interfere with their own break. Green and Reese decided that rather than going down the wall, as they had planned, they would join the other men and escape through the tunnel.

At the far end of the cells were funnel shaped openings. They were only four by twelve inches on the outside, but two feet square on the inside. A shutter could be opened for ventilation or closed to keep out the cold air. The men tried to widen these openings, but the rocks were too firmly placed and too hard. The rock floor, however, was made of pumice. The damp Perote climate had made it soft, so the Texans were able to cut into it.

After some work, it was possible for a man to crawl into the space in the thick wall that was between the opening in the cell and the outside opening. The Texans kept the shutter closed and took turns lying flat on their stomachs and chiseling through the rock with whatever slight and crude instruments they could manage. John Taney, the whistler, was now nicknamed "The Gopher" because of his speed and skill in digging.[1]

Only sixteen men attempted the escape through the tunnel. Many prisoners did not join because there were rumors that Santa Anna was going to release them all soon. Others felt that their chances of success were too slim to merit the risk. Yet others simply didn't know about the plans. The castle was enormous, and the men were kept busy. They had little contact with other Texans except the ones who were confined with them each night.

Five men in the center room where the tunnel was being dug decided not to attempt escape. They traded places with men from the other rooms who were going. Switching cells put them at risk since the guards would certainly know that these men had known about the tunnel.

The Texans chose the rainy night of July 2, 1843, to make their break. Because of the foul weather, the Texans weren't asked to line up for a head count outside their cell doorways. Instead the cold and careless guards glanced into the cells for their hasty count.

Green and Odgen had slipped into the center cell rather than going to their own. They lay in the shadows with blankets drawn closely about them. Tecolote Trimble pointed to them and called to the guard that they were sick. The guard did not check further.

A group of prisoners started playing a card game near the door of their cell and involved the guard in their game. They had a jug of mescal, and using an egg shell for a cup, they passed drinks through the grill to the guard. To cover the noise of digging, prisoners sang, danced, and rattled their chains to Tecolote Trimble's square dance call. When one pair of dancers wore out, another would take their place, and each dance ended with the hoot of an owl or the crow of a rooster. The party had to last a long time because the hole the men had made turned out to be too small. It took two more hours of frantic digging to get it big enough.

The smallest men went first, since a large man might get stuck in the hole and keep the others from escaping. The first escapee was John Twohig, the storekeeper who, when Woll captured San Antonio, blew up his own building so the

Mexicans couldn't get supplies. He went feet first into the hole, pulling his knapsack after him. Because of his small size and high energy, he had done the most work on the tunnel. One by one the others squeezed through and went down a rope hand over hand. Isaac Allen lost his grip and fell, but he landed in ankle deep sand.

Samuel Stone was a large man, and he got stuck. He couldn't move either way. His cell mates slid a rope to him and, sweating and straining, finally managed to pull him back into the cell. Even after that ordeal, he didn't give up. He said, "I have a wife and children at home, and I would rather die than stay here longer: I will go through, or leave no skin upon my bones."[2] He stripped and tried again naked. This time he made it, pulling his clothes behind him.

It took three hours to get all the men out. Then they stole across the moat bridge. Once they were across, they split into groups of twos and threes and set out in different directions, all hoping to make their way to the coast.

The next morning, in order to give the escaped men a little more time, the remaining prisoners did not file out of their cells as usual. Putting themselves at risk of severe punishment, they called out one excuse after another. When the guards went in to see what was really wrong, they found that sixteen men were gone.

Green Makes It

Green left a note behind addressed to General President Santa Anna. He said that the climate of Perote did not suit his health so he had retired to one in Texas that was more agreeable to his feelings.

Most of the escaped prisoners didn't get far. John Young fell off a cliff and injured himself so badly he was easily recaptured. He was back within a few hours. Eight of the sixteen were back in chains within a few weeks.[3] Samuel Stone, Isaac Allen, and John Taney were among them.[4] After this escape, all the prisoners were closely watched.

Green and Daniel Drake Henrie took the road toward Veracruz. They were overtaken by Reese, Twohig, and John Dalrymple.

The fortunate Green had American friends in Mexico City, and they arranged help for him along the way. In Jalapa, Green, Reese, Dalrymple, and Henrie stayed with an elderly Mexican who was opposed to Santa Anna's government. Then, to get over the mountains, they were guided by bandits who led them on secret trails by night and hid them in bushes by day. When they reached Veracruz, a Frenchman hid them in his inn until they could catch an American steamer for New Orleans. Twohig hired on a Mexican war steamer that was bound to the United States. It took him to Charleston, South Carolina.

In September 1843, Green had made it all the way back to Brazoria County. He was greeted as a hero. It had been one year since the volunteers had first gathered outside San Antonio. He wrote a journal in which he glorified himself and attacked Sam Houston. His comments about John C. C. Hill, however, show the general respect given the boy by the Texans. Green's lack of resentment toward John C. C.'s privileged treatment also seems to be typical. He wrote, "He frequently visited us in our confinement, expressing the keenest solicitude for our welfare and the more earnest hopes of our speedy deliverance. . . . He behaved with the gallantry of a veteran throughout the bloody fight."[5]

CHAPTER 41

Captives Are United at Perote

General Thomas Jefferson Green was already at home in Texas when the Texans from Molina del Rey arrived at Perote Castle on September 21, 1843. Twenty-one were sick and had remained at Molina del Rey.

The Perote prisoners were shocked to see the Molina del Rey men. James L. Trueheart, one of the Perote prisoners, wrote in his diary:

> We were much surprised to see their haggard looks and miserable appearances, most of whom were dressed as Mexican Comanches, without shoes or shirts. My feeling in thus beholding my countrymen was oppressive in the extreme. Their whole appearance indicated to me the effects of bad treatment and hard usage.[1]

Edward Manton wrote home to La Grange, "Big Wallace . . . looks very thin, although in good health. They have worked him thin a carrying sand on the road at Mexico."[2]

The Texans from Molina del Rey made similar comments about the men who had been in Perote. "The sad countenances and wasted appearance of these men but too well attested the sufferings of their long imprisonment."[3]

Despite the recent escape, the guards humanely gave the newcomers all the privileges they could and left them unchained for a month. Even though the newcomers must have longed for the open sky of Molina del Rey, they were glad to have the chance to talk with the other Texans. They swapped tales and enjoyed each other's company, although the Texans were still given barely enough food to keep alive. Anyone who wanted more than starvation fare had to buy it. John Taney said he often wished he were some good man's dog so he would have enough to eat.[4]

Lice

The men badly needed fine-toothed combs, which had to be bought. Bigfoot Wallace lost his in the escape at Salado, and years later he spoke of it as a severe loss. The Texans had already been suffering from parasites, and now they were in a castle that was infested with lice. The floors where they slept were cleaned with boiling water every day, but every morning the prisoners awoke covered with the creatures.

The Texans, determined not to give in to low spirits, had louse races, picked favorites, and bet on them. When a favorite louse got ahead, they cheered; when it fell behind, they groaned.

The Mexican guards at Perote, like their fellows at Molina del Rey, discovered that giving rewards was the best way to manage the Texans. One favorite reward was to be allowed to go to a sunny spot in the prison yard and scout each others' heads for lice.

Typhus

Only four days after their arrival at Perote, the men began to suffer from headaches. These were followed by chills and fever. The Texans referred to the illness as *prison fever*. They thought it was the result of being closed up with poor ventilation and poor food. There was no way for air to get into their cells except through the single door, which was often kept closed, and through a small vent in the outside wall. The prisoners were forced to breathe "the putrid air of a room in which thirty men were confined."⁵ Moreover, the rooms were cold and damp, and the hungry men's few clothes were threadbare. These conditions were enough to cause sickness. However, the disease was probably typhus, and was caused by lice. The epidemic spread to the guards, to their families, and into the village.

The Mexicans attempted to control the epidemic. They put wooden planking on the floors so the men didn't have to sleep on the cold stones, and they began to keep the doors of their cells open all day for better ventilation. They also limited water, eliminated fruit, and added *chili con carne* to the men's diets.

Joseph D. McCutchan was the first to fall ill. He lay in the hospital for thirty days and was unconscious fourteen of them. He described his recovery as "death itself, though in a different, more horrible shape.... Give me death itself in any shape, save from that disease."⁶

James L. Trueheart wrote that the disease began with pain in the arms and legs and a severe headache. Delirium and almost total weakness followed. He later wrote, "... I laid like a dead man for nearly 20 days, neither speaking, hearing, nor seeing, and insensible to everything. The disease is usually attended with pain in the limbs, violent headache, producing in a very few days delirium, and complete prostration, ..."

Every day ox carts crossed the drawbridge taking fevered and delirious men to the hospital. October, November, and December were cold. Although rain and hail fell almost daily, patients were carried to and from the hospital on open litters. Sometimes the ox carts came back with a body wrapped in blankets and bound with twine, ready to be buried in the castle moat. Since so many Texans were sick, those who were chained two by two had their chains separated. Each man carried his own chain.

The hospital itself seemed like a mad house. Blisters rose on the sick men's bodies. They twisted and screamed in pain. At the height of his delirium, Bigfoot became entirely unmanageable and fought all the attendants at the hospital. They had to lasso him and tie him down. This wasn't easy, for as Bigfoot said, he was no chicken at ordinary times, and his strength was magnified by his delirium.[7]

One day, after Bigfoot's frenzy had calmed, an attendant came in to dress his blisters. The attendant handled Bigfoot in a cruel way, and hurt him badly. There was a heavy copper stew-pan within Bigfoot's long reach. He seized it and bashed the attendant in the head. The man fell to the floor, out cold.

The guards rushed at Bigfoot with their sabers drawn. Bigfoot said he would soon have been mincemeat if the surgeon general had not stepped in and stopped the guards. The surgeon said the attendant was a brute and deserved just what he got. The surgeon and Bigfoot became personal friends, and he gave Bigfoot a present of money and clothes. Bigfoot remembered him fondly many years later, saying he hoped the surgeon lived a thousand years and never lost his front teeth.[8]

Man's Inhumanity to Man

The ordeal of the epidemic brought out the worst in human nature. Fights broke out among the Texans. One man actually refused to give a dying comrade twelve cents for food.[9] The guards took advantage of the prisoners' weakness, and for the first time physical abuse was common. Several men wrote in their journals about seventeen-year-old Gilbert Brush being cruelly beaten with an oak stick.

Depression and Suicide

All but three of the Texans came down with the disease. Twenty died. The surviving prisoners returned from the hospital weak and depressed. Many gave in to self-pity. Disease had robbed them of what no other hardship had been able to take away—their humor.

Campbell Davis, who had suffered for months with chronic diarrhea was almost a skeleton even before he fell ill with typhus. He was kept in the hospital for forty days. When he was sent back to the prison, he managed to get into a doctor's medicine. He drank a bottle of laudanum and died later that day.[10] After he took the laudanum, he said that if it were to do over, he would act the same. He was the only Texan to commit suicide. "I have lost all hope of recovering, I cannot recover—and in fact either a life of sickness or health, is not to be coveted here. I wish I could die!"[11] McCutchan praised Davis as a "good man," a "boon companion," and a "noble defender," and dropped "o're him a soldier's tear."[12]

Norman Woods and Tecolote Trimble Die

One wonders if Tecolote Trimble, the natural mimic and clown, managed to keep his humor to the end. He died in the epidemic. So did his friend and neighbor, Norman Woods.

Woods died December 13, 1843.[13] Probably none of the Texans had suffered more than he did, and surely none showed more bravery. To the end, he wrote letters of hope and courage to his wife and brother. In his last letter, he said, "I have never despaired" and signed it, "Yours until death, Norman Woods."[14]

He was a gallant Texan.

CHAPTER 42

Release of the San Antonio Prisoners

The fate of prisoners rests on politics, and in this respect the Mier men were at a disadvantage. Even though Mexico did not recognize the Republic of Texas and regarded it as a part of Mexico that was in revolt, a dialogue was established. Mexico and Texas agreed to a year of peace.

The Texas prisoners hoped to be released as a result of the armistice, but Santa Anna realized that they were a good bargaining chip so he kept them locked up. When he discovered that the armistice had simply been a way to distract attention from Sam Houston's secret negotiations for Texas to become part of the United States, Santa Anna had no reason at all to release the men.

About this time, the Texans' great champion, Maverick's cousin, Waddy Thompson, resigned his position as United States minister to Mexico. Before he returned home, he went to visit President Santa Anna at his estate near Jalapa. The two men had learned to respect each other during Thompson's service, and because of their personal relationship, Thompson decided to raise the question of releasing the prisoners one last time.

Santa Anna replied, as he had many times, that the Texans were not men of their word. He had released the Santa Fe prisoners on the condition that they never take up arms against Mexico again. They had sworn an oath that they would not, but they returned to fight again almost immediately.

He also said that the Mier men were nothing but robbers. They had invaded Mexico for plunder, and they didn't deserve freedom. Thieves in Mexico who had committed crimes far less serious than the sack of Laredo were in prison. The Texans were being treated fairly.

Waddy Thompson had to recognize that Santa Anna's arguments regarding the Mier men were strong, so he turned his attention to the men who had been captured by Woll in San Antonio. He repeated Maverick's argument that these men were not robbers; they had been defending their homes. Santa Anna acknowledged that this was true. He signed an order for the release of the San Antonio prisoners and of the Dawson prisoners as well. On March 24, 1844, the remaining Texans who had been captured in San Antonio eighteen months earlier in the Woll incursion were released. Waddy Thompson said, "Nothing could have been more handsome than the way in which this was done and I am sure I never experienced a more heartfelt pleasure."[1]

Some of the other Texans, including John Taney, the whistler, tried to pass themselves off as part of the San Antonio group. But the trick didn't work.

For reasons that are unclear, both Milvern Harrell, Norman Woods' faithful nephew, and young Allen H. Morrell, were released. Morrell went by ship to New Orleans. There, ragged and penniless, he asked some ministers for help, and they gave him lodging and money to return to his home and his father, Zenos Morrell. His mother, grieving over his imprisonment, had died while he was in Perote.

CHAPTER 43

Bigfoot Is Freed

Bigfoot Wallace's father persuaded some influencial men to exert pressure for Bigfoot's release.[1] They did, and on August 5, 1844, Bigfoot and three other Texans were released.[2]

With one dollar each, Bigfoot Wallace and his companions set out in the broiling sun, walking toward Veracruz. Mexicans treated the three kindly on the road. "One woman gave Wallace water and fanned him when he came to her door nearly dead with heat after a long tramp across a sandy plain."[3] They passed through Jalapa, which Wallace declared had the finest climate and the loveliest women in all Mexico.

A few miles from Jalapa, they were stopped by eleven *bandidos* who demanded their money. Bigfoot told them they had just been liberated from prison and were not "flush with money."[4] He showed them his passport, signed by Santa Anna. The *bandidos* then called Santa Anna a scoundrel and wanted to know why the Texans hadn't killed him. Bigfoot said, "If I had had the keeping of him he would not trouble Mexico any more," a reply that "seemed to tickle them amazingly."[5]

The *bandidos* kept the Texans company on the road, took them to a ranch, and served them a good supper. Bigfoot told them that if that was their usual style of living, he would like to join their group. The next morning the *bandidos* gave them food for their trip and sent them on their way.

When at last they reached Veracruz, yellow fever was raging. People were dying by the hundreds. The men waited eleven days and finally caught a ship, the *Creole*. It was contaminated with yellow fever and had been condemned, but they were so eager to get home, they took it anyway. When the captain learned the Texan's story, he generously refused to charge them for the trip.

They all came down with yellow fever, but survived and made it to New Orleans. Bigfoot Wallace signed on the police force there and in three weeks made more than enough money for the rest of his trip.

CHAPTER 44

The Men Left Behind

Finally the imprisoned men lost all hope. The Mier men had long thought that the Republic of Texas would somehow see to it that they were let out of prison. They saw their attack at Mier as a patriotic deed that would be supported by their fellow countrymen. They did not take into account, any more than they had when they set out, that Texas had no army and no money. They also seem not to have taken into account that the Texans back home knew little about what had happened to them and had their hands full already. Indians and robber gangs threatened them. They struggled to make a living and to build a society. They had to establish laws and create communities with churches and schools.

The Texans had pinned their hopes on being freed after the armistice between Mexico and Texas. When that failed, they hoped for an act of generosity from Mexico. It was a time when leaders were often generous for emotional rather than logical reasons, and the Mier survivors built their hopes for release on the thinnest of straws. Santa Anna's saint's day, June 13, was looked forward to with anticipation. He might free prisoners on that day. The day came and went. No release order came.

At last, months spent sick and in chains with too little food and finally with too little hope, caused the Mier men to act desperately. Alfred Thurmond, the interpreter who had to translate the sentence of the Black Bean decimation and Ewen

Cameron's death sentence, and who had witnessed Cameron's brave death but managed to keep his spirit strong, now broke. In full view of the guards, he suddenly threw down his shovel and ran. They brought him back, bleeding and in double irons.[1] Fire eater Gilbert Brush broke away from his guards in broad daylight when he was hauling stones. He was also retaken.[2]

CHAPTER 45

Doña Inés de Santa Anna Dies

On August 23, 1844, before Bigfoot had gotten out of Mexico, Santa Anna's wife, Doña Inés, died. She was thirty-three years old. Santa Anna mourned her death with a procession of 20,000 mourners[1] led by Archbishop Posada, who conducted her funeral in the cathedral. John C. C. Hill was among the mourners. She had been tender and motherly to him, and he had confided in her. It could only have been a painful loss to a youth who had already lost many friends.

The Mexican people turned out *en masse* to honor her. They regarded her as an example of the finest womanly virtues. Even the Texan prisoners held her in high esteem.

Rumor has it that Doña Inés' dying request was that Santa Anna free the Mier men. Perhaps this is true. Perhaps it simply suited the sentimental temper of the time to think so. Or perhaps it is an extension of the Texans' many comments about the kindness of Mexican women.

CHAPTER 46

Santa Anna Is Persuaded

Wilson Shannon, the new U.S. minister who had taken Waddy Thompson's place, arrived in Mexico City on August 26, 1844. He had been robbed[1] in broad daylight two miles outside Puebla. On arriving in Mexico City, he found that because of the death of Donna Iñes, he could not see Santa Anna at once, so he went to Perote to see the Texas prisoners. He was horrified at their condition. Several had been beaten, and all had been almost starved for more than a month. They were given only enough food to keep them alive — small amounts of rotten potatoes, musty rice, and bad meat. Shannon told them he would do everything he possibly could to help them.

John Taney[2] and the other prisoners in cell number seven answered that they had already made another tunnel and would be escaping soon. Shannon asked them to let him try to persuade Santa Anna to release them. They agreed to wait.[3]

A few days later, on September 5, 1844, Shannon met with Santa Anna and presented his credentials. He also handed Santa Anna a letter urging the release of the Mier prisoners. Santa Anna replied, "I have liberated many of the Texian Prisoners . . . and now only those are retained in prison who . . . have attempted to escape, assassinating the Mexican soldiers who guarded them. These criminals deserve death."[4]

Soon Shannon requested another interview and again asked for the release of the Mier men. He did not try to justify their actions, but he emphasized that they were a matter of great concern to the United States and that their release might have a favorable influence on the relationship of the two countries. He probably also suggested that releasing them could have a favorable effect on settling Mexico's debt to the United States. Santa Anna agreed to release all Texans in prison in Mexico except for the last of the Santa Fe expedition men — Jose Antonio Navarro,[5] who he regarded as a traitor. Shannon did not argue.

Why Did He Do It?

After resisting for so long, why did Santa Anna suddenly agree to release the Mier men? We can only speculate. Even John C. C. was often puzzled by Santa Anna's complex nature that blended brutality with kindness. U.S. minister Wilson Shannon had presented reasonable arguments, but they were not new to Santa Anna, and Mexico and the United States were on the brink of war. Perhaps Santa Anna may have simply wanted to get off on the right foot with the new U.S. minister, or perhaps he thought that the Texans had served enough time.

Another possible reason for the release relates to a scandal that had caused a sensation in the international press. It involved General Ampudia — he who lost his son in the battle at Mier and who first extended kindness to John C. C. Hill.

General Ampudia was put in command of the Mexican forces at Yucatán shortly after his victory at Mier. In early June of 1843, General Francisco Sentmanat appeared in Yucatán with fifty men. He had earlier opposed the current Mexican regime and had been sent into exile. Now he seemed to be back to raise a rebellion.

Sentmanat's group was captured. They surrendered their arms, but Ampudia had thirty-eight of them executed. Most of those who were killed were foreigners, including several French and Spanish citizens and three U.S. citizens. This caused tensions with all of those countries. To make matters worse, General Ampudia had Sentmanat shot and his head cut off. His head was then fried in oil and displayed in an iron cage for several days. The entire civilized world was horrified.

It is difficult to understand how General Ampudia, who was so loving to John C. C., so generous to the other fire eaters, and so kind to all the Texans in his command, could have done such a thing. It should be remembered that Yucatán was full of violence, both Indian and Creole. General Ampudia may well have been attempting to use terror to maintain control.

As a result of General Ampudia's shocking act, Santa Anna removed him from his position as commander of the forces in Yucatán. It may be that Santa Anna released the Mier men in an attempt to soften the bad impression of Mexico Ampudia had caused.[6]

We can never be sure how much each of these events contributed to Santa Anna's decision, but at 6:00 P.M. on September 14, 1844, he signed the document ordering their release. Ironically, in only six weeks, Santa Anna himself would fall in a revolt and would himself be imprisoned in Perote.

Still Defiant

When the news of Santa Anna's decision reached Perote,

Yucatán

Yucatán was torn by a racial-civil war between the Mayan Indians and the Mexicans of European descent, known as Creoles. It continued for many years. In 1848 the governor offered to give the entire state of Yucatán to any government that would save the Creoles. No one accepted the offer. The Creoles were almost all driven from the area, but they returned, well armed. They burned Mayan villages and reconquered the Yucatán peninsula. Half the Mayan population died and most of the others were driven into rain forests. Yucatán was filled with violence, and it suffers from political and social turmoil to this day.

the men sang and danced until almost dawn. That morning, they were made to report to duty as usual, and they were afraid they would not be freed after all. However, the official order arrived in the evening, and their chains were taken off. Their deep, running sores and their deep bitterness remained.

John Taney, the whistler, and some of the other Texans had managed several times during their captivity to cut off their chains and to hide them so well that the guards couldn't find them. Before the Texans were released, the guards asked where the chains were hidden, but the Texans refused to tell. They did not want them used on some other poor souls.[7]

At three o'clock in the afternoon on September 15, 1844, 104 Texan prisoners were marched into the plaza. They were the last of the 258 men who fought at Mier.[8] A light rain was falling. General Jarero and the Mexican garrison, in full dress uniform, told them goodby. Some of the Mexicans with whom the Texans had formed friendships hugged them. The Mexican women who ran the stores and who had shown them so much kindness were also at the farewell ceremony. In the commandant's office, lit by two small candles on a table beside a Bible and crucifix, the Texans swore an oath never to fight Mexico again. Some of the Texans raised their left hands, some muttered, some did not speak at all. The Texans signed the document, but in their hearts they vowed revenge.

The Texans had been in captivity one year and seven months. So threadbare they were almost naked, they took their dollars and started their long way home. The Mier men's imprisonment was finally over.

CHAPTER 47

What Happened to John C. C. Hill and Bigfoot Wallace?

John C. C. Hill (1828-1904)

John C. C. lived a charmed life. He studied at the *Mineria*, was put in charge of his dormitory, and later became a professor of English there. While Donna Iñes was alive, he visited her and General Santa Anna each Sunday afternoon and joined them on drives or visiting friends in the palace. During the Mexican American War, John C. C. found himself busy helping both sides in humanitarian ways. His influence, at age eighteen, saved the Mineria College from the invading American soldiers.

John C. C. met a lovely English girl named Mary Murray. Mary's mother had recently died of yellow fever, and her father was very protective. John C. C. and Mary fell in love. They met frequently at her home and at the home of American friends. Her father heard that they were planning to marry in secret. Although Mary denied this, her father decided to take her away. He rented a ship and sent Mary and her sister and brother to California to stay with a friend. Although John C. C. wrote Mary, the father didn't give the letters to her and wrote John C. C. telling him not to write any more. Mary thought John C. C. had been killed because a ship that was on the way to California was sunk, and she believed John C. C. was on it.

In 1850, John C. C. graduated with honors in civil and mining engineering. He continued graduate studies at the University of Mexico. He was appointed to a position as mining engineer at the San Miguel and Regla silver and gold mines. While working there, he met Augustina Sagredo of Real del Norte, daughter of a general and niece of Raymon Sagredo, a prominent artist. Thirteen years after John C. C. rode off with the volunteers, he returned to Texas to ask his parent's blessings on his marriage to Augustina. The blessings were gladly given, and the couple were married in 1855. They had four children.

John C. C. was strongly in favor of political reform and was concerned about educating the Mexican people and raising the general standard of living. Although he had good relations with many people who had different political opinions, he was criticized by many others. He was threatened because of his work for the poor. He was given the name *Paño de Lagrimas* or *Handkerchief for Tears* because of his efforts to comfort and aid the poor.

After the overthrow of Santa Anna, when Benito Juarez became president of Mexico (1858-1872) he worked for reforms that John C. C. agreed with: freedom of religion, surrender of land by the church, free public schools, and individual rights. John C. C. also later supported Jose Porfirio Diaz. Nevertheless, he maintained his personal relationship with Santa Anna.

John C. C. saw Santa Anna sent to Perote, and saw Maxmillian's court rise and fall (1864-1867). Shortly after Maxmillian became Emperor of Mexico, all those who opposed him were charged with treason. Captain Ampudia, brother of General Ampudia who first befriended John C. C., was condemned to death. John C. C. obtained permission to take Captain Ampudia's sweetheart to the prison for a final visit. During the visit, they dressed the captain in a dress and rebozo they had smuggled in. John C. C. led the "girl" out, her head covered in her rebozo as though overwhelmed by grief. So Captain Ampudia escaped. They were not afraid for the life of his sweetheart because her brother was on Maxmillian's side, and while he couldn't free Captain Ampudia, he could protect his sister.

As a mining engineer, John C. C. was involved in lead, zinc, coal, and silver mining. As a civil engineer, he helped to lay out railway lines. In addition, he became a practicing physician.

John C. C.'s wife, Augustina, died in 1897. His son Angelito had died in 1856 when he was not yet a year old. His sons, Alberto (b 1863) and Carlos (b 1867) and his daughter, Maclovia (b 1856) lived to adulthood.

John C. C. had warm relationships with all his family. He often visited Texas and wrote frequently to his relatives, who also visited him in Mexico.

After the death of Augustina, it happened that Hamlin Garland, the famous journalist, was in Mexico. He interviewed John C. C. and wrote an article about him which appeared in *McClure's Magazine*. In one of the incredible strokes of fate that were typical of John C. C.'s life, Mary Ann Murray Masterson, the widowed sweetheart of his youth, saw the article and wrote to John C.C. They were married in 1898.

John C. C. died in Monterrey, Nuevo Leon, Mexico, in 1904, having lived seventy-six very full years.

William Alexander (Bigfoot) Wallace (1817–1899)

Colorful, big-hearted Wallace, a descendant of the Scottish Highlanders William Wallace and Robert Bruce, rejoined the Texas Rangers as soon as he was released from Perote. He was with the Rangers during the Mexican-American War. Later he was captain of his own Ranger company and was an expert at trailing. He also drove a mail hack from San Antonio to El Paso. During the Civil War his task was to guard the frontier against the Comanches. He never married. The state of Texas granted him a little ranch on the Medina River.

Although Bigfoot inherited substantial property in Virginia, he never claimed it. Wharton J. Green, son of Thomas Jefferson Green, visited him in San Antonio and tried to get him to claim his inheritance, estimated at between $50,000 and $100,000, which was a fortune indeed in those days. Bigfoot said:

> Why don't I go and get it? Simply because I don't want it. What use would it be except to make me miserable? I'm tolerably well satisfied over yonder, beyond the Medina, by myself. My rifle and traps furnish all I need for meat, and the peltries my other little wants, such as powder, lead, coffee ... What more does a man require to make him happy? And yet you ... would have me break up a life that suits me and take to one that I hate and despise. A big house ... with lots of pretended friends as long as the money held out. Wouldn't I be a fool to make the swap?"[1]

He spent his later years in Frio County where a small village, Bigfoot, is named for him.

Whatever Bigfoot did was made memorable by his exuberant personality. Two incidents from the Mexican-American war are recorded:

> Bigfoot was in all the fighting at Monterrey and in the assault on the bishop's palace where his captain was killed. At the end of the battle while the bugles were sounding and the Mexicans were surrendering, Bigfoot aimed his gun at a Mexican who had a flag. U.S. officers intervened.
>
> "Lieutenant, don't you know a parley when you hear it sounded?" one of them asked.
>
> "Not when I am in front of *that* man," Wallace answered. He then angrily asked the Mexican if he had a bean lottery there. He held up his hand and said, "Look at that hand. Do you know it? Ever see it before?"
>
> The Mexican said, "No."
>
> "You have, and called upon others to look at it."[2]
>
> It was the very man who had held the bean pot when the

Texans drew for their lives. Bigfoot cursed him for all the low-down Mexican cowards in the calendar, and then let him go.

During the storming of Monterrey, the Texas troops stopped at the Hidalgo Hotel to look for food, but the provisions had been taken. A tiny Mexican man told the men that for a dollar he would bring them a blanketful of bread. Bigfoot gave him a dollar and told him to "skin out and git it."[3] The little man came back promptly with a bundle of as much bread as he could carry. One of the Texans said he was afraid the bread might be poisoned. Bigfoot called the Mexican, picked up a loaf that had some cracks in it, and told him to eat it. The Mexican didn't want to eat, but Bigfoot aimed his revolver at him and cocked it. The man took the dry loaf and started eating it. When he finally got it down, Wallace picked out another loaf and told him to eat it. The poor little Mexican rolled his eyes and made signs that he was choking to death. The Texans gave him a quart of water and put the bread in his hand. He soon choked, but Bigfoot gave him more water. Then he encouraged him by pointing the pistol at his eye. When he finished the loaf, the Mexican smiled, but his face soon fell when Bigfoot handed him another loaf. Before he took it, the Mexican made the sign of the cross and called on a saint. Whenever he choked, Bigfoot would give him more water, and the Mexican would look at the pistol. When the third loaf was eaten, Bigfoot told him to sit still awhile and see if it would kill him. After two minutes, he showed no signs of sickness, and the Texans ate. The kind little Mexican left, declaring that he couldn't eat again for a week.[4]

Other Survivors: (See details of each man below)

1. Alexander, John Rufus
2. Brush, Gilbert
3. Chalk, Whitfield
4. Fisher, William S.
5. Green, Thomas Jefferson
6. Hays, Jack
7. Harrell, Milvern

8. Hill, Asa
9. Hill, Jeffrey Barksdale
10. Maverick, Samuel Augustus
11. Morgan, John Day
12. Morrell, Zenos
13. Oldham, William
14. Phelps, Orlando
15. Reese, Billy
16. Sellers, Harvey
17. Somervell, Alexander
18. Walker, Sam

Alexander, John Rufus (1817-1908). Alexander was the great-grandson of John Adams, second president of the United States. He was one of the four men who escaped at Salado and made it home, and was the only one to record his experiences. He was the last survivor of the Mier men and is buried at Round Mountain, Texas.

He was tall, broad shouldered, heavy limbed, sinewy, with a large head, crowned with an immense shock of very fine, curly hair, light brown in his youth, grey but still thick and curly in his age. After the Mier Expedition he went to Fayette County, married Mary Fisher Jones, and settled down to rear a family of eleven children. In 1861, at the age of forty-three, John Rufus Alexander enrolled as a private in the Civil War. He was in a volunteer infantry company known as the Dixie Grays. "The infirmity that afflicted his great-grandfather, John Adams, in his extreme old age" came on him, too. (Wade 12) He was almost blind in 1879, and was completely so for the last twenty-seven years of his life. (Wade 14)

Brush, Gilbert. In spite of his especially miserable time on the Mier expedition, Gilbert Brush returned to fight in the Mexican War. He was wounded at Monterrey.

Chalk, Whitfield (1811-1902). After hiding in the oven at Mier and successfully making his way back to Texas, Whitfield Chalk lived a full and productive life. In 1844 he was elected major of the Second Regiment of the First Militia

Brigade and served for two years. He fought in the Mexican War as a private in the Texas Rangers. He was later sheriff of Williamson County. With his brother, he founded a lumber mill on Salado Creek. He was awarded $402.50 and 320 acres of land for his service on the Mier Expedition. He married in 1847 at the age of thirty-six, and fathered nine children. A marker was erected on his grave with full military honors from the United States government.

Fisher, William S. (? -1845). After his release from Perote in 1843, Fisher returned to his home in Jackson County, Texas, where he died two years later.

Green, Thomas Jefferson (1802-1862). After escaping from Perote and returning to the Republic of Texas, Green served in the Texas Congress as representative of Brazoria County. He moved to California in 1849 and served in the First Senate there. He sponsored the bill that created the University of California, and he became a major general of the California militia. In his later years he returned to his native North Carolina and settled on a plantation where he died at the age of sixty-one, heartbroken over the reverses of the Confederacy.

Hays, Jack (1817-1883). The able, fearless Jack Hays, "Devil Yack," had a full life and a stellar career. He moved from the rank of captain to major in the Texas Rangers and gained a national reputation in the Mexican war. In that conflict, he headed the First Regiment, Texas Mounted Riflemen; his regiment scouted and took part in the attack on Monterrey in 1846 with General Zachary Taylor. Hays' second regiment kept lines open between Veracruz and Mexico City for General Winfield Scott. After the Mexican War, Hays pioneered trails through the Southwest. He was appointed Indian agent for Gila River country; was elected sheriff of San Francisco County in 1850; and was later appointed United States surveyor general. He was one of the founders of the city of Oakland and was successful in real estate and ranching. Hays was neutral in the Civil War. He married in 1847 and had three sons and three daughters.

Harrell, Milvern (1825-1910). Milvern Harrell, the nephew who so faithfully took care of Norman Woods and who repeated came so close to death, lived a long life. His memories of his time in Mexico were published in the *Dallas Morning News* on June 16, 1907.

Hill, Asa (1788-1844). Asa Hill was released and reached Galveston on August 20, 1843. From there he made his way home to La Grange. He never recovered from his long ordeal. He died July 15, 1844, at the age of 56.

Hill, Jeffrey Barksdale. Jeffrey Hill who seems to have borne suffering with such patience, is the forgotten man of the Hill family. Although we found records about the other brothers, we found no information about Jeffrey. It seems that he lived and died quietly without calling attention to himself.

Maverick, Samuel (1803-1870). After his release from Perote, Sam Maverick served in the Eighth Congress of the Republic of Texas. He strongly advocated annexation to the United States and after that was accomplished, served in the fourth through ninth state legislatures. He worked for equal opportunity for all his constituents and worked to ensure a fair and efficient judicial system. He opposed secession from the union, but ultimately threw his support to the Confederacy. During the war he was elected chief justice of Bexar County and served as mayor of San Antonio. He was survived by his wife and five of his ten children.

The term *maverick*, meaning an unbranded calf and suggesting a person who goes his own way, is taken from Sam Maverick's habit of letting his cattle roam unbranded. He considered any animal without a brand to be his. At the time of his death, Sam Maverick owned more than 300,000 acres of land.

Morgan, John Day (1819-1899). In spite of suffering on the Santa Fe and Mier expeditions, John Day Morgan went against the Mexicans again in the Mexican War. He drove a commissary wagon in Major General Zachary Taylor's army. However, he quit after three months to go back to his parents' home in Cincinnati, Ohio, where he married Rebecca Rogers.

In a few years, he returned to Texas with his wife and established a farm west of Bastrop. They had five children.

Morrell, Zenos N. (1803-1883). Although Zenos N. Morrell moved to Texas in 1835 because of weak, bleeding lungs, he lived a long, active life. He devoted himself to founding Baptist churches and to other religious work. He also fought Indians, speculated in land, taught school, and engaged in business, but without financial success. His wife Clearancy, the mother of his four children, died in 1843, perhaps because of grief for Allen Morrell who was imprisoned in Perote. Zenos married a widow, Delia Harlan, in 1845. Zenos' duties for the Mission Board of the Southern Baptist Convention required that he make a round-trip of 300 miles on horseback from Cameron to Corsicana. His wife could not tolerate his constant absences, and they divorced after fifteen years of marriage. Morrell did missionary work in Honduras, and in his later years devoted himself to writing. His most notable work is *Fruits and Flowers from the Wilderness*, originally published in 1872 and recently reissued by Eakin Press.

Oldham, William (1798-1868). Oldham was described in the *St. Louis Globe Democrat* as "a born leader, possessing the courage and endurance of a Spartan." After his escape from Salado, Oldham returned to his home, known as "Fort Oldham" in Burleson County. He was called on by the settlers to fight Indians at Battleground Prairie in 1844. This was the last major fight with Indians in the county. Oldham acquired extensive land and developed a plantation in the Brazos bottom. In 1860, he was listed as one of the three wealthiest men in Burleson County. He died without a will, and his relative, W. S. Oldham Jr., of Houston, was appointed to administer his estate. W. S. Oldham maintained that William Oldham had no wife or children, but a beautiful mulatto named Phyllis said that she had been his wife since 1839 and that she had borne him six sons. W. S. insisted that she was just a slave and evicted her and her sons from the plantation. She sued the estate and was finally awarded homestead rights. She and the children returned to the plantation where they and their descendants continued to live.

Phelps, Orlando. Orlando remained in Brazoria County. He left several children.

Reese, Billy (1826?-1851). Billy Reese returned to Mexico to fight again in the Mexican War, as did his brother, Captain Charles Keller Reese. They both fought at Monterrey. Billy married and emigrated to California.

Sellers, Harvey (1827-1874). Harvey served with Jack Hays' Regiment of Texas Rangers in the Mexican War. He fought in the battle of Monterrey. He settled in Houston and was in business until 1851 when he moved to New York and joined the firm of Bowman, Sellers & Company. He returned to Texas at the onset of the Civil War. He moved steadily up in rank and was ultimately a Colonel. At the second battle of Manassas, he commanded the left wing of Hood's army and was afterwards recommended by General Longstreet for promotion to Brigadier. After the Civil War, Sellers returned to New York and became a partner in J. H. Brower & Co. He helped establish the first regular steamship line between Galveston and New York. In 1867 he returned to Galveston and went into the cotton business. He was founder of the Merchants' Insurance Company of Galveston, helped organize the Galveston New Wharf and Cotton Press Company and the Galveston Cotton Exchange. He was the first president of the exchange. He died suddenly in Galveston on April 10, 1874 at the age of forty-seven.

Somervell, Alexander (1796-1854). Alexander Somervell, leader of the bungled Somervell expedition, was rewarded for his services by being appointed collector of customs for the port of Calhoun. He helped develop the town of Saluria on Matagorda Island between 1845 and 1847. In February of 1854 he was murdered, and the killer is unknown. Somervell's body was found tied to the timbers of a capsized boat. He had been on his way from Lavaca to Saluria and was carrying a large amount of money.

Walker, Sam (1817-1847). After his escape from Perote

and his successful return to the Republic of Texas, Sam Walker joined Hays and his Rangers. He fought at the famous battle of Walker's Creek near the Pedernales River. In that battle, fifteen rangers, using new Colt revolvers, defeated about eighty Comanches. Although quiet and modest, Walker's "daredevil disregard for his own safety" won him admiration and fame. "War was his element . . . the battlefield his playground." (Haynes 20 and note 34) He enlisted as a private in the U.S. Army under General Zachary Taylor in 1845. The next year he formed his own company. Walker was an outstanding scout and was presented a horse by the citizens of New Orleans in thanks for his brave deeds. He was lieutenant colonel in the Texas Mounted Riflemen in the Mexican War and fought in the battle of Monterrey. He went to Washington, D.C., to recruit for his company. During that excursion, he visited Samuel Colt. Walker proposed improvements to the revolver, and the newly designed six-shooter was called the Walker Colt. While in Mexico, he was stationed in Perote to fight guerillas. He grew embittered and violent, and seldom took prisoners. He was killed in an assault at Huamantla on October 9, 1847. He was thirty years old.

Woods, Henry Gonzalvo (1816-1869). Gonzalvo, Norman Woods' beloved brother, responded to Norman's letter asking that he care for the family he had left behind. Gonzalvo married Norman's widow, Jane, on October 30, 1844. He raised Norman's five children and four of his own. He became a successful rancher and horse-breeder. He built the first sawed-lumber two-story home in DeWitt County and brought the first cotton gin and the first cook stove to that area. He enlisted in the Confederacy in 1863.

In the fall of 1869, Gonzalvo was deputized to chase an alleged murderer named John Kerlick. He was ambushed and killed by Kerlick on November 28, 1869.

Time Line

September 11, 1842	Sam Maverick and others captured by General Woll.
Mid September 1842	The Hills, Woods, Zenos Morrell, Bigfoot, and others band together in Seguin to go to San Antonio and rescue the captives
September 17, 1842	Battle of Salado River
September 17, 1842	Dawson battle
September 19, 1842	General Woll leaves San Antonio with the captives. Hays, Caldwell, and their men attack Woll's army at the Hondo
October 4, 1842	Maverick learns of Joe Griffin's death at the Dawson battle
October 1842	Houston appoints Somervell to lead the expedition to rescue the captives
November 4, 1842	Somervell arrives at the volunteers' camp and orders the troops to wait for the cannon. Harsh winter sets in.
November 23, 1842	The march to Mexico begins.
November 1842	Dawson prisoners (Woods, Harrell, MacCreadae, and Patterson) attempt to escape.
December 1842	Sack of Laredo

Time Line

December 19, 1842	Somervell Expedition ends.
December 22, 1842	Maverick and the other San Antonio captives arrive at Perote Castle.
December 25, 1842 afternoon:	Texan spies enter Mier to reconnoiter.
night:	Texans enter Mier and take cover in houses.
December 26, 1842	Battle begins before sunrise. Texans inflict enormous casualties and then surrender.
January 9, 1843	Mier prisoners arrive in Matamoros
January 12, 1843	Generals Fisher and Green leave Matamoros
January 14, 1843	Mier prisoners leave Matamoros in chains
January 30, 1843	Generals Fisher and Green arrive in Saltillo
February 11, 1843, early	Generals Fisher and Green leave Haciendo de Salado for Mexico City under Captain Romero's guard.
February 11, 1843, breakfast:	Texans escape from Hacienda de Salado
February 21, 1843	Recaptured Texans are taken back to Saltillo.
March 1843	John C. C. Hill arrives in Mexico City.
March 11, 1843	John Day Morgan, Jeffrey Barksdale Hill, and four other prisoners who had been wounded set out for Mexico City via Tampico to join the other prisoners.
March 22, 1843	Maverick, Jones, and Judge Hutchinson taken to Mexico City.
March 25, 1843	Black Bean episode

March 30, 1843	Maverick, Jones, and Hutchinson officially released.
Late March 1843	Green and Fisher arrive at Perote Prison.
April 1843	Alexander and Oldham return to San Antonio.
April 23, 1843	John Day Morgan, Jeffrey Hill, and the other four prisoners arrive in Tampico.
April 24, 1843	Ewen Cameron executed. Franklin Chase, U.S. Consul visits the prisoners in Tampico.
May 4, 1843	Maverick returns to San Antonio.
May 22, 1843	Orlando Phelps, freed by Santa Anna, arrives in New Orleans.
July 2, 1843	Green and others escape from Perote Prison.
July 31, 1843	Ranger Sam Walker escapes from Molina del Rey.
August 25, 1843	John Day Morgan escapes from Molina del Rey.
September 1843	Green arrives in Brazoria County, Texas.
September 21, 1843	Molina del Rey prisoners transferred to Perote.
March 24, 1844	Last of the San Antonio captives released; also Milvern Harrell and Allen Morrell.
August 5, 1844	Bigfoot Wallace released.
September 14, 1844	The last 104 Mier men are released.

Endnotes

Chapter 1: Before the Capture
1. In her journal, Mary Maverick, wife of Sam Maverick, aged thirty-nine and the former mayor of San Antonio, described how their Tejano friends came to tell them that an invasion was likely and that they should run to safety. Nance, Joseph Milton, *Attack and Counterattack: The Texas-Mexican Frontier, 1842* (Austin: University of Texas Press, 1964) p. 9n, from Rena Maverick Green (ed.), *Memoirs of Mary A. Maverick: Arranged by Mary A. Maverick and Her Son George Madison Maverick*, p. 60.
2. Nance, *Attack and Counterattack*, 454.
3. Winkler, E. W., ed, "The Bexar and Dawson Prisoners," *Texas Historical Association Quarterly* 13 (1909-1910), 295.
4. The name Apache most probably came from the Zuñi word apachu, meaning "enemy." The Apaches referred to themselves as Inde or Diné, meaning "the people." The Apaches went by numerous names. Because of their nomadic nature, it seems probable that several names were used to identify the same band. Two groups, the Lipans and the Mescaleros, lived partially or entirely within the confines of Texas.
   The social unit of the Lipan and Mescalero Apaches was the extended family. Several extended families generally stayed together and were led by their most prominent member, who acted as chief advisor and director of group affairs. A number of the groups lived in close proximity and could unite for defensive or offensive purposes, or for social or ceremonial occasions. The leader of the combined groups was the band leader. The Lipans had no formal organization larger than the band. This loose organization caused problems in relations with the Spanish, and later with the Mexicans, Texans, and Americans. One Apache band, for instance, might make peace with its enemies, while another would remain at war.
   When Texas gained its independence, relations between whites and Apaches were relatively cordial. The Texans drew up their own treaty with the Lipans in 1838, but the alliance broke down in 1842. Some 250 of the approximately 400 Lipans left Texas for Mexico, where they joined the Mescaleros on destructive raids across the border for several decades. In 1873, Col. Ranald S. Mackenzie led a force of 400 soldiers into Mexico to destroy the Lipan villages. His army killed or captured virtually all of the sur-

viving Lipans. Thirty-five Lipans were living in Oklahoma in 1940 but were not officially listed among the tribes of the state.

Drawn from "Apache Indians" by Jeffrey D. Carlisle. http://www.tsha online.org/handbook/online/articles/AA/bma33.html. Accessed November 27, 2009.

5. Webb, Walter Prescott. *The Texas Rangers, A Century of Frontier Defense* (Austin: University of Texas, 1935, 1965) 15.

Chapter 2: Texans Before the Capture

1. Hill in Bartlett 20; Hill in Gooch-Iglehart 32.

The quotations in this entire section and all the information about John C. C.'s decision to join the volunteers are drawn from these two sources. John C.C. himself reported this information in detail directly to Bartlett and to Gooch-Iglehart.

2. Woods in Paul Nuckols Spellman, "Zadock and Minerva Cottle Woods, American Pioneers," Master's thesis, University of Texas at Austin, 1987, 129.

3. The Muster Oak is located at the intersection of Washington and Colorado streets in La Grange, across from the Fayette County Courthouse. This gathering was probably the first recruitment of citizen soldiers under the famous tree. See http://famoustreesoftexas.tamu.edu/TreeHistory.aspx?TreeName=Muster+Oak. Accessed October 18, 2009. © 2005 Texas Forest Service.

4. Caldwell consistently spelled his first name with one *t:* Mathew. Nance, *Attack and Counterattack*, 336n.

5. Morrell, Zenos N. *Flowers and Fruits of the Wilderness* (Waco: Baylor University Press, 1976), 161.

6. Morrell, *Flowers and Fruits*, 161.

7. Ibid.

8. Sowell, Andrew Jackson, *Texas Settlers and Indian Fighters of Southwest Texas* (Austin: State House Press, 1986), 420.

9. The description of Flacco is drawn from three sources: Caperton, John. *Sketch of Colonel John C. Hays, Texas Ranger.* (Transcript in A.L.U.T.); Gooch-Iglehart, Fanny Chambers, *The Boy Captive of the Texas Mier Expedition* (J. R. Wood: 1909); and Greer, James Kimmins. *Colonel Jack Hays Texas Frontier Leader and California Builder*. College Station: Texas A&M University Press, 1987. (Originally New York: Dutton, 1952).

10. Webb, *The Texas Rangers*, 56

11. Gooch-Iglehart, *The Boy Captive*, 58, 88; Greer, *Colonel Jack Hays*, 29-30; Morrell, *Flowers and Fruits*, 168-176.

12. Nance, *Attack and Counterattack*, 447n, from Smithwick, *The Evolution of a State*, 221-224.

13. Marks, *Turn Your Eyes Toward Texas*, 106, from Weyland and Wade, *Fayette County*, 156-157.

14. Slavery was outlawed in Mexico in 1828.

15. Marks, *Turn Your Eyes Toward Texas*, 106, from Green, *Memoirs*, 69; Nance, *Attack and Counterattack*, 372n.

Chapter 3: The Battle of Salado

1. Ramsay, James to Miles S. Bennet 1882 from Manuscript of the Mexican War as quoted in Republic of Texas-Index/Captain Adam Zumwalt-Battle of Salado, p.10, http://www.tamu.edu/ccbn/dewitt/salado.htm. Accessed 10/16/98.

2. Morrell, *Flowers and Fruits*, 169.

3. Nance, *Attack and Counterattack*, 360, from Thomas Jefferson Green 168.

4. Republic of Texas-Index/Captain Adam Zumwalt-Battle of Salado, p. 5 http://www.tamu.edu/ccbn/dewitt/salado.htm. Accessed 10/16/98

5. Sowell, A. J. 1884 from Rangers and Pioneers of Texas as quoted in Republic of Texas-Index/Captain Adam Zumwalt-Battle of Salado, p. 12 http://www.tamu.edu/ccbn/dewitt/salado.htm. Accessed 10/16/98.

6. All quotations in the scene with Bigfoot and Whaling are from Day, *Black Beans and Goose Quills*, 132 ; the same quotations are used in Sowell, *Early Settlers*, 59.

7. Sowell, *Early Settlers*, 316.

Chapter 4: The Dawson Massacre

1. Morrell, *Flowers and Fruits*, 171.

2. Wade 157.

3. Weyland and Wade, *Fayette County*, 155.

4. Nance, *Attack and Counterattack*, 366. In a note on the same page, Nance quotes Paul R. Spellman: "The Woods boys always resented any implication that any of them were opposed to fighting on this occasion."[Spellman to Houston Wade, San Antonio, Texas, Sept. 5, 1934, in Houston Wade Papers, ms.] If true, this is quite amazing as Norman Woods' reasonable assessment of the situation seems to have been the one example of good judgement shown.

5. The site of the Dawson fight is in present day San Antonio. In 1936 during the Texas centennial celebrations, a marker was erected at the side of the Austin-San Antonio highway, a mile from the battleground. The site of the battle is on Houston Street where it joins the Missouri-Kansas-Texas Railroad. Nance, *Attack and Counterattack*, 366n.

6. Nance, *Attack and Counterattack*, 372, from Thomas Jefferson Green, p 167.

7. Smithwick, *The Evolution of a State*, 190.

8. Sinks, *Chronicles of Fayette*, 67.

9. Sowell, *Early Settlers*, 817.

10. The quote might be apocryphal. Nance, *Attack and Counterattack*, 372, from A. A. Gardenier to the Editor of the *Telegraph*, La Grange, Oct. 21, 1842, *Telegraph and Texas Register*, Nov 16, 1842.

Nance points out in a note that Gardenier's account of the Dawson fight is based largely on Henry Gonzalvo Woods' account of the occurrences. However, the Woods brothers' accounts disagree. In a letter to Gonsalvo, Norman Woods said that it was Carrasco who ordered that the prisoners be executed and Woll who gave the order to spare their lives. Nance, *Attack and Counterattack*, 376, Norman Woods to H. G. Woods, Molino del Rey,

July 5, 1843, in L. U. Spellman (ed.) "Letters of the 'Dawson Men' from Perote Prison, Mexico, 1842-1843" *SHQ* 38 (1934-1935), 257-259. This is an example of how confusing and contradictory even first-hand information about a battle can be. These two accounts were by brothers who were both participants.

11. Morrell, *Flowers and Fruits*, 173.

12. Wade reports thirty-nine killed in the fight and gives the following survivors and what happened to them:
    (1) Barclay, Richard A. (Escaped from Perote July 2, 1843)
    (2) Bradley, John (Released from Perote, Sept. 22, 1843)
    (3) Coltrin, William (Died at Perote January 27, 1844)
    (4) Faison, Nathaniel W. (Released from Perote March 24, 1844)
    (5) Harrell, Milvern (Released from Perote, March 25, 1844)
    (6) Higgerson, John (Killed in Salado break Feb. 11, 1843)
    (7) Kornegay, David Smith (Escaped from Perote July 2, 1843)
    (8) Manton, Edward T. (Released from Perote March 23, 1844)
    (9) McCrady, John (Drowned in Rio Grande, Nov. 1, 1842)
    (10) Morrell, Allen H. (Released from Perote March 23, 1844)
    (11) Patteson (Drowned in Rio Grande, Nov. 1, 1842)
    (12) Robinson, Joseph C. (Released from Perote March 23, 1844)
    (13) Shaw, Joseph (Released from Perote March 23, 1844)
    (14) Trimble, William James (Died in Perote Jan. 5, 1844)
    (15) Woods, Henry Gonzalvo (Escaped from fight)
    (16) Woods, Norman B. (Died in Perote, Dec. 16, 1844)

13. Morrell, *Flowers and Fruits*, 171.

14. Spellman, Paul N. *SHQ*, 134.

15. Morrell, *Flowers and Fruits*, 172.

16. Ibid. The unnamed man was killed in the Battle of Salado. He had left his horse tied carelessly some distance from the other horses. Some Indians who were with the Mexican army went toward his horse, and the unfortunate man left his post against his captain's orders to try to get his horse. He killed three Indians in the fight that followed, but the Indians finally killed him. This all occurred in his comrades' clear view. They were forbidden to go to his aid because he had disobeyed orders. This is ironic indeed, since none of the Texans were noted for obeying orders.

17. Sowell, *Early Settlers*, 817.

18. Morrell, *Flowers and Fruits*, 173. Morrell refers to this lady as "the English minister's wife, Mrs. Elliot." However, as an anonymous reader was kind enough to point out, the British *chargé d'affairs*, Charles Elliot, lived in Galveston, so it seems unlikely that the lady Morrell refers to was his wife. She might have actually been Mrs. William Elliot, Mary Maverick's friend.

19. Morrell, *Flowers and Fruits*, 175.

20. Ibid.

Chapter 5: Disgrace at the Hondo

1. Sowell, *Early Settlers*, 68.

2. Greer, *Colonel Jack Hays*, 76.
3. Sowell, *Big Foot*, 68.
4. Sowell, *Early Settlers*, 27.
5. Ibid., 22.
6. Green, *Samuel Maverick*, 171.
7. Jenkins, *Recollections of Early Texas*, 112.
8. Cutrer, *Ben McCulloch*, 56.
9. Nance, *Attack and Counterattack*, 396. He draws from Chabot's comments in Trueheart's diary, the 1924 edition, pp. 56-58.

Chapter 6: San Antonio Captives
1. Marks, *Turn Your Eyes Toward Texas*, 109.
2. Ibid., 108.
3. Ibid., 108.
Maverick later sent a "fine set of China to Madame Taylor in remembrance of her kindness." Mrs. Albert Maverick reported that the boy who brought fruit later moved to San Antonio. He told her that as long as Sam Maverick lived he sent him a suit of clothes every Christmas. Marks, *Turn Your Eyes Toward Texas*, n283.
4. Nance, *Dare-Devils*, 117.

Chapter 7: The Republic of Texas Challenges Mexico
1. Erath, *Memoirs of George B. Erath*, 65.
2. Haynes, *Soldiers of Misfortune*, 16, Houston to Santa Anna quoted from Houston Writings 2: 526-527.
3. Erath, *Memoirs of George B. Erath*, 66. George Bernard Erath states that the following year Sam Houston told him what his instructions had been. They were: "to proceed with extreme caution to the Rio Grande, to cross it only when there was no possibility of an obstruction to recrossing, and to venture no general or partial action unless victory was certain in advance. The intention was to make a demonstration—to show the world we could occupy the country we claimed and beyond it, and to maintain our occupation longer than the Mexicans could occupy our own soil."

Chapter 8: At the Camp
1. Erath, *Memoirs of George B. Erath*, 64. "We collected with difficulty about two hundred beeves whose owners, I suppose, received pay for them some ten years later when we had money."
2. Haynes, *Soldiers of Misfortune*, 39.
3. Haynes, *Soldiers of Misfortune*, 43, from Llerena B. Friend, ed., "Sidelights and Supplements on the Perote Prisoners," *SHQ* 68:369.
4. Duval, *Big-Foot Wallace*, 167.
5. McCutchan, *Mier Expedition Diary*, 38n.

Chapter 9: On the Trail—Bog, Drought, Flood, and Stampede
1. Haynes, *Soldiers of Misfortune*, 47, from McCutchan, *Mier Expedition Diary*, 17.

2. The Atascosa bog is beside the Atascosa River. "Rancho del Atascoso, sometimes called El Atascoso ("bog"), was an outlying ranch of San José y San Miguel de Aguayo Mission. The ranch lay astride the Atascosa River between the sites of present day Pleasanton and Poteet in Atascosa County. It derived its name from the deep sand in the area." Rancho de Atasecosa, Robert H. Thonhoff, *Handbook of Texas online*. http://www.tshaonline.org/handbook/online/articles/RR/aprrr.html. Accessed December 26, 2009.
3. Bartlett, *Those Valiant Texans*, 28 n 4.
4. Erath, *Memoirs of George B. Erath*, 67.
5. Greer, *Colonel Jack Hays*, 83.

Chapter 10: Laredo
1. Nance, *Attack and Counterattack*, 511.
2. Hendricks, "The Somervell Expedition," *SHQ* 23:127.
3. Jenkins, *Recollections of Early Texas*, 133.
4. Bell, *A Narrative of the Capture*, 10.
5. McCutchan, *Mier Expedition Diary*, 25.
6. Haynes, *Soldiers of Misfortune*, 56; Elliot to Addington, November 15, 1842, No. 13, British Diplomatic Correspondence Concerning the Republic of Texas, 127.

Chapter 11: Somervell Finale
1. Haynes, *Soldiers of Misfortune*, 59, from Green, *Journal of the Texas Expedition*, 61-62.
2. Erath, *Memoirs of George B. Erath*, 68.
3. Wade, *Notes and Fragments*, 21.
4. Erath, *Memoirs of George B. Erath*, 70.
5. "It was stamped at the time as unofficer-like conduct in Gen. S. to presume to march the command home without adequate supplies and horses—many of the men being on foot and others with weak horses, utterly unable to perform the trip—when, too, we were surrounded by an abundant commissariat department [Mexico]. Major J. D. Cocke to _____, Matamoros, Jan. 12, 1843, reprinted from the *New Orleans Bulletin* in the *Morning Star* (Houston), March 4 and 7, 1843. The letter was endorsed by Edwin [Ewen] Cameron, John R. Baker, Claudius Buster, William M. Eastland, J.G.W. Pierson, Charles K. Reese, William Ryon, and Israel Canfield, who were described as "captains." Nance, *Attack and Counterattack*, 561.
6. McCutchan, *Mier Expedition Diary*, 32.

Chapter 12: The Expedition Divides
1. Nance, *Dare-Devils All*, 15.
2. Nance, *Attack and Counterattack*, 567, as taken from Stapp, *Prisoners of Perote*, 30.
3. Cutrer, *Ben McCulloch*, 61.
4. Greer, *Colonel Jack Hays*, 89.

5. Haynes, *Soldiers of Misfortune*, 64, from Sterling Brown Hendricks, "The Somervell Expedition," *SHQ* 23:138.
6. Bartlett, *Those Valiant Texans*, 38.
7. Haynes, *Soldiers of Misfortune*, 63, from *Telegraph and Texas Register*, January 14, 1846.
8. McCutchan, *Mier Expedition Diary*, 45.

Chapter 13: Cuidad Mier at Last
1. Marks, *Turn Your Eyes Toward Texas*, 111.
2. Joe Franz estimates the distance in his introduction to William Preston Strapp, *The Prisoners of Perote*.
3. Bartlett, *Those Valiant Texans*, 39.
4. Bartlett, *Those Valiant Texans*, 40.
5. Nance, *Dare-Devils All*, 46.

Chapter 14: The Mexican Forces
1. Haynes, *Soldiers of Misfortune*, 68, from "Triunfo sobre los Tejanos," *Politico Semanario*, December 29, 1842.
2. Gooch-Iglehart, *The Boy Captive*, 128.

Chapter 15: Before the Battle
1. Bartlett, *Those Valiant Texans*, 38.
2. All the dialogue in this scene is drawn from Bartlett, *Those Valiant Texans*, 44. Although Bartlett gives these direct quotations, it seems unlikely that they could be accurate.
3. Bartlett, *Those Valiant Texans*, 45-46.
4. Ibid., 46.
5. Wade, *Notes and Fragments*, 24.
6. McCutchan, *Mier Expedition Diary*, 44-45.
7. Nance, *Dare-Devils All*, 54.

Chapter 16: The Battle at Cuidad Mier
1. Jenkins, *Recollections of Early Texas*, 112.
2. Webb, *The Texas Rangers*, 87.
3. Sowell, *Big Foot*, 75.
4. Gooch-Iglehart, *The Boy Captive*, 123.
5. Wade, *Notes and Fragments*, 25.
6. Gooch-Iglehart, *The Boy Captive*, 121.
7. Bartlett, *Those Valiant Texans*, 50.
8. Jenkins, *Recollections of Early Texas*, 109.
9. Nance, *Dare-Devils All*, 61; Duval, *Big-Foot Wallace*, 176.
10. McCutchan, *Mier Expedition Diary*, 48.
11. McCutchan, *Mier Expedition Diary*, 58-59.
12. Nance, *Dare-Devils All*, 58.
13. Bartlett, *Those Valiant Texans*, 51.
14. Nance, *Dare-Devils All*, 61.
15. Bartlett, *Those Valiant Texans*, 52.

16. Erath, *Memoirs of George B. Erath*, 75.
17. Haynes, *Soldiers of Misfortune*, 73, from *Telegraph and Texas Register*, August 2, 1843.

Chapter 17: Surrender
1. Haynes, *Soldiers of Misfortune*, 73, from *Telegraph and Texas Register*, August 2, 1843. Haynes' note 30 lists numerous other sources as well.
2. Nance, *Dare-Devils All*, 75.
3. Thomas Jefferson Green 217.
4. Gooch-Iglehart, *The Boy Captive*, 127.
5. Bartlett, *Those Valiant Texans*, 60.
6. Ibid.
7. Nance, *Dare-Devils All*, 32.
8. Nance, *Dare-Devils All*, 70 from Green 101.
9. Wade, *Notes and Fragments*, 27.
10. Bartlett, *Those Valiant Texans*, 59.
11. Both of these quotations are from Bartlett, *Those Valiant Texans*, 61.
12. Nance, *Dare-Devils All*, 71, 72.
13. Duval, *Big-Foot Wallace*, 170.

Chapter 18: John C. C. and General Ampudia
1. Gooch-Iglehart, *The Boy Captive*, 136-150. All the narrative from the point of John C.C.'s breaking his gun is drawn from Gooch-Iglehart as told to her in person by John C. C. Hill.
2. Bartlett, *Those Valiant Texans*, 60.
3. Both quotations are from Thomas Jefferson Green 106.

Chapter 19: After the Battle
1. Wallace in Sowell, *Big Foot*, 81. However, an anonymous scholar who was kind enough to review the manuscript for Texas Tech University Press called the figure of 800 absurd. "The battle was fought almost entirely in close quarters, house to house fighting. For purposes of contrast, 600 Mexicans were killed by a much larger Texas army in open terrain at San Jacinto. This is an example of the lengths to which the Mier prisoners were willing to go to explain away their defeat."
2. Sowell, *Big Foot*, 81.
3. Nance, *Dare-Devils All*, 91, from Duval, *Big-Foot Wallace*, 181.
4. Nance, *Dare-Devils All*, 72, from Jenkins, *Recollections of Early Texas*, 134.
5. All the dialogue with the wounded men is drawn from Gooch-Iglehart, *The Boy Captive*, 153-160; John C. C. Hill reported it to her.

Chapter 20: Flacco Is Murdered
1. Nance, *Attack and Counterattack*, 576 from John Henry Brown, *Indian Wars and Pioneers of Texas*, 573-574.
2. Smithwick, *The Evolution of a State*, 162.
3. Ibid. That there should be a letter from Navarro strikes us as extremely odd since Navarro was in prison in Mexico.

4. Smithwick, *The Evolution of a State*, 162.

Chapter 21: The Captive Mier Men on the Road
1. Day, *Black Beans*, 78.
2. McCutchan, *Mier Expedition Diary*, 68.
3. Nance, *Dare-Devils All*, 95.
4. Ibid., 102, from *Daily Picayune*, Jan 26, 1843.
5. Day, *Black Beans*, 78.
6. Nance, *Dare-Devils All*, 98.
7. Ibid., 100, from McCutchan's *Narrative*, 67; Walker, *Account*, 39.
8. Day, *Black Beans*, 78 .
9. Nance, *Dare-Devils All*, 105.
10. McCutchan, *Mier Expedition Diary*, 68.
11. Nance, *Dare-Devils All*, 102, from *Daily Picayune*, Jan 26, 1843.
12. Haynes, *Soldiers of Misfortune*, 99, from Stapp, *Prisoners of Perote*, 51.
13. Duval, *Big-Foot Wallace*, 205.
14. McCutchan, *Mier Expedition Diary*, 70.
15. Wade, *Notes and Fragments*, 29.

Chapter 22: Texans Start for Mexico City
1. McCutchan, *Mier Expedition Diary*, 71 (endnote).
2. Ibid.
3. Haynes, *Soldiers of Misfortune*, 102, from Green, *Journal of the Texas Expedition*, 132-134.
4. All of the quotations in this paragraph are taken from Thomas Jefferson Green 136.
5. Nance, *Dare-Devils All*, 113.
6. Winkler, 299; Nance, *Dare-Devils All*, 113n.
7. Spellman, ed., "Letters of the Dawson Men" SWHQ 38 (April 1935) 264-265.
8. Wade, *Notes and Fragments*, 32.
9. Day, *Black Beans*, 13.
10. Nance, *Dare-Devils All*, 216.
11. Wade, *Notes and Fragments*, 35.

Chapter 23: Texans Make a Break
1. Wade, *Notes and Fragments*, 1:52.
2. Haynes, *Soldiers of Misfortune*, 104, from Canfield, "Israel Canfield," *TMH* 3:176; Hunter 6.
3. Nance, *Dare-Devils All*, 219.
4. Ibid., 220.
5. The quotations in this paragraph are drawn from McCutchan, *Mier Expedition Diary*, 84.
6. Sowell, *Early Settlers*, 84.
7. Nance, *Dare-Devils All*, 223, from Sowell, *Early Settlers*, 68.
8. Day, *Black Beans*, 131.

9. Wade, *Notes and Fragments*, 35.
10. Nance, *Dare-Devils All*, 222; Walker, *Account*, 45.
11. Nance, *Dare-Devils All*, 223; Sowell, *Early Settlers*, 68.
12. Ibid.

Chapter 24: Thomas Jefferson Green Uses Suasion
1. Gooch-Iglehart, *The Boy Captive*, 250; Nance, *Dare-Devils All*, 225. Nance attributes to Fisher the words Gooch-Iglehart attributes to Green. Nance is the more scholarly source, but Gooch-Iglehart's account is fuller and more detailed, and as Thomas Jefferson Green is more prominent in this narrative, we used her version. Also, Green is often seen to use words effectively. We have found no other incident that suggests that Fisher was eloquent.

Chapter 25: After the Battle at Hacienda de Salado
1. At Hacienda de Salado, several of the sick prisoners had been put in separate quarters. One of these was Benjamin Z. Boone, grandson of Daniel Boone. John R. Baker, wounded in the battle, came bleeding into the sick room, lay down beside Boone, and told him about the break. Weak as he was, Boone rose from his sick bed, bid his wounded comrade good-bye, and joined the escaping Texans. [In a speech given on December 12, 1970, James M. Day dismissed this story, told to A. J. Sowell by Boone, as "the account of an old man basking in reflected glory." Day's opinion was that Boone was too sick to have participated in the escape. We found no clear support for either version.]
2. Nance, *Dare-Devils All*, 238.
3. Wade, *Notes and Fragments*, 37.
4. Haynes, *Soldiers of Misfortune*, 107.
5. Duval, *Big-Foot Wallace*, 199.
6. Duval, *Adventures*, 204.
7. Nance, *Dare-Devils All*, 240, from Stapp, *Prisoners of Perote*, 60.
8. Nance, *Dare-Devils All*, 249, from Duval, *Big-Foot Wallace*, 200.
9. Nance, *Dare-Devils All*, 241; The accounts of who gave the men a guide and directions are confusing. Nance says it was Ewen Cameron's relative and refers to him as an Englishman. Haynes simply calls him an Englishman with no reference to Ewen Cameron. Haynes draws from Stapp's *Prisoners of Perote*, p. 75 and Bell's *A Narrative of the Capture*, pp. 29-30. Nance credits Samuel H. Walker's *Account*, p. 49.

Chapter 26: In the Mountains
1. Wade, *Notes and Fragments*, 42.
2. Bartlett, *Those Valiant Texans*, 105.
3. Nance, *Dare-Devils All*, 246, from Duval, *Big-Foot Wallace*, 203.
4. Nance, *Dare-Devils All*, 248, from Woodland "The Story of the Massacre of Mier Prisoners," *Houston Daily Post*, Aug. 16, 1891, p. 8, col. 1.
5. Duval, *Big-Foot Wallace*, 210, Claudius Buster to John H. Jenkins [n.p., n.d.,] in Wade, *Notes and Fragments*, 76.

6. Day, *Black Beans*, 132.
7. Nance, *Dare-Devils All*, 248.
8. Wade, *Notes and Fragments*, 77.
9. Ibid., 48.
10. Duval, *Big-Foot Wallace*, 208.
11. Wade, *Notes and Fragments*, 45.
12. Ibid., 50.
13. Ibid., 48.
14. Ibid., 54.
15. Balmony (*Chelone glabra*), commonly called snakehead, is a very bitter herb with a flavor like black tea. It acts mainly as a tonic for the liver and digestive system, and has a laxative effect. Bown, D. *Encyclopaedia of Herbs and their Uses*. Dorling Kindersley, London, 1995.
16. Wade, *Notes and Fragments*, 59.
17. Ibid., 57.
18. Nance, *Dare-Devils All*, 255.
19. Haynes, *Soldiers of Misfortune*, 115, from Hunter, John Warren, "Adventures of a Mier Prisoner: Being the Thrilling Experiences of John Rufus Alexander, Who Was with the Ill-Fated Expedition Which Invaded Mexico." Bandera: *Frontier Times*, n.d.
20. Wade, *Notes and Fragments*, 63.
21. Thomas W. Cox, a Baptist lay preacher, and John D. L. Blackburn were among the fortunate. Blackburn's feet were bare, and so cut and sore he could hardly walk. Cox was a large man, and he carried Blackburn on his back as much as he could. They reached Cox's home in LaGrange only eighteen days after the Salado break, and Cox, a man of great eloquence, impressed listeners with his description of their adventures.

Chapter 27: Recapture
1. Jenkins, *Recollections of Early Texas*, 113.
2. Nance, *Dare-Devils All*, 262, Canfield diary, February 18, 1843; Stapp, *Prisoners of Perote*, 66-67.
3. *Pobrecito* means "poor little thing."
4. Duval, *Big Foot Wallace*, 21.
5. Nance, *Dare-Devils All*, 282, from Stapp, *Prisoners of Perote*, 70-71.
6. Wade, *Notes and Fragments*, 83.
7. Ibid., 84.

Chapter 28: The Black Bean Episode
1. Nance, *Dare-Devils All*, 283, from Sowell, *Early Settlers*, 23.
2. Sowell, *Big Foot*, 94.
3. Nance, *Dare-Devils All*, 286.
4. Ibid.
5. Eastland, William Mosby, by Thomas Cutrer, *The Handbook of Texas Online*, http://www.tshaonline.org/handbook/online/articles/EE/fea7.html. Accessed January 9, 2010.
6. Eastland, William Mosby, by Thomas Cutrer, *The Handbook of Texas*

Online, http://www.tshaonline.org/handbook/online/articles/EE/fea7.html. Accessed January 9, 2010.
   7. Nance, *Dare-Devils All*, 289, from Sowell, *Early Settlers*, 74.
   8. Thomas Jefferson Green, 170.
   9. Wade, *Notes and Fragments*, 50.
  10. Thomas Jefferson Green, 172.
  11. Nance, *Dare-Devils All*, 290.
  12. "Whalen, Henry A." by Thomas Cutrer, *Handbook of Texas Online* http://www.tshaonline.org/handbook/online/articles/WW/fwh87.html. Accessed January 9, 2010.
  13. Thomas Jefferson Green, 172.
  14. Thomas Jefferson Green, 173.
  15. Nance, *Dare-Devils All*, 290.
  16. Thomas Jefferson Green, 172.
  17. Sowell, *Early Settlers*, 74.
  18. Duval, *Big-Foot Wallace*, 233.
  19. Sowell, *Early Settlers*, 74.
  20. Duval, *Big-Foot Wallace*, 232.
  21. Gooch-Iglehart, *The Boy Captive*, 268-269.
  22. Ibid.
  23. Ibid.
  24. Bell, *A Narrative of the Capture*, 52.
  25. Nance, *Dare-Devils All*, 294, from Canfield's diary, March 25, 1842; account of Charles Keller Reese, *Northern Standard*, February 10, 1844.
  26. Haynes, *Soldiers of Misfortune*, 126, from Lord, *Frontier Times* 15:549.
  27. Jenkins, *Recollections of Early Texas*, 113.
  28. The men decimated at Mier were:
             (1) Cash, John L.
             (2) Cocke, James D.
             (3) Dunham, Robert Holmes
             (4) Eastland, William Mosby
             (5) Este, Edward E.
             (6) Harris, Robert
             (7) Jones, Thomas L.
             (8) Mahan, Patrick
             (9) Ogden, James M.
             (10) Roberts, Christopher
             (11) Rowan, William
             (12) Shepherd, J. L.
             (13) Thompson, J. N. McDonald
             (14) Torrey, James N.
             (15) Turnbull, James
             (16) Whaling, Henry
             (17) Wing, Martin Carrol

Chapter 29: Survivors March On
   1. Jenkins, *Recollections of Early Texas*, 114.

2. Haynes, *Soldiers of Misfortune*, 128, from Stapp, *Prisoners of Perote*, 97.
3. Sowell, *Big-Foot*, 77.
4. Ibid., 100.
5. Bartlett, *Those Valiant Texans*, 107.
6. Sowell, *Big-Foot*, 101.
7. Day, *Black Beans*, 133.
8. Ibid.
9. Ibid.

Chapter 31: John C. C. Hill
1. Bartlett, *Those Valiant Texans*, 87.
2. Gooch-Iglehart, *The Boy Captive*, 230; Bartlett, *Those Valiant Texans*, 119.
3. Bartlett, *Those Valiant Texans*, 119.
4. Gooch-Iglehart, *The Boy Captive*, 233.
5. Ibid., 238.
6. Ibid., 234.

Chapter 32: Maverick in Perote
1. Marks, *Turn Your Eyes Toward Texas*, 105.
2. Ibid., 112.
3. Ibid., 113.
4. Ibid, 115.
5. Ibid, 115.
6. Ibid, 116.

Chapter 33: Green's Group Arrives at Perote
1. Day, *Black Beans*, 78.
2. Nance, *Dare-Devils All*, 417.
3. McCutchan, *Mier Expedition Diary*, 110.
4. Haynes, *Soldiers of Misfortune*, 144, from Peter Maxwell to Samuel Walker, October 18, 1843, Thomas Jefferson Green Papers.
5. Haynes, *Soldiers of Misfortune*, 142, from Green, *Journal of the Texas Expedition*, 320-322.

Chapter 34: The Fire Eaters Arrive in Mexico City
1. Bartlett, *Those Valiant Texans*, 125-126.
2. Ibid., 127.
3. Ibid., 138.
4. Nance, *Dare-Devils All*, 420.
5. Nance, *Dare-Devils All*, 420, from Green, *Mier Expedition*, 259.

Chapter 35: Asa Hill's Decision
1. Haynes, *Soldiers of Misfortune*, 130.

Chapter 36: The Prisoners at Molino Del Rey
1. Haynes, *Soldiers of Misfortune*, 135, from Stapp, *Prisoners of Perote*, 117.
2. Bartlett, *Those Valiant Texans*, 132.
3. Haynes, *Soldiers of Misfortune*, 135.

Chapter 37: Letters Home
1. McCutchan, *Mier Expedition Diary*, 80.
2. Bartlett, *Those Valiant Texans*, 144.

Chapter 38: Escapes from Molina del Rey
1. Spellman, L. U., "Letters," 263.
2. Ibid., 267.
3. Ibid., 265.
4. Ibid., 265.
5. McCutchan, *Mier Expedition Diary*, 80-81.

Chapter 39: Escape from Perote
1. Haynes, *Soldiers of Misfortune*, 160-161.
2. Haynes, *Soldiers of Misfortune*, 161.
3. Sowell, *Early Settlers*, 79.
4. Duval, *Big-Foot Wallace*, 235.
5. Jenkins, *Recollections of Early Texas*, 138.

Chapter 40: Captives are United at Perote
1. Smithwick, *The Evolution of a State*, 205.
2. Nance, *Dare-Devils All*, 173 from Green 316-317. However, according to Haynes, *Soldiers of Misfortune*, 164, it was Isaac Allen who got stuck and had to take off his clothes in order to get through the tunnel.
3. Haynes, *Soldiers of Misfortune*, 164.
4. Nance, *Dare-Devils All*, 179 from Trueheart, *Diary* July 12, 1843; Haynes, *Soldiers of Misfortune*, 164; Smithwick, *The Evolution of a State*, 205.
5. Bartlett, *Those Valiant Texans*, 140.

Chapter 41: Release of the San Antonio Prisoners
1. Nance, *Dare-Devils All*, 347 from Trueheart diary, Sept 21, 1843.
2. Nance, *Dare-Devils All*, 347 from Edward Manton to Hezekia Smith, Castle of Perote, September 22, 1843 (By the politeness of Mr. Bradley), in Edward Manton Papers (photostat), TxU-A.
3. Nance, *Dare-Devils All*, 347 from Trueheart diary, Sept. 21, 1843.
4. Smithwick, *The Evolution of a State*, 205.
5. Nance, *Dare-Devils All*, 350, from Bell, *A Narrative of the Capture*, 75.
6. Day, *Black Beans*, 24.
7. Duval, *Big-Foot Wallace*, 238.
8. Ibid., 240.
9. Haynes, *Soldiers of Misfortune*, 169, from Canfield, "Israel Canfield" *TMH* 3:195.
10. Haynes, *Soldiers of Misfortune*, 181, from Canfield, "Israel Canfield" *TMH* 3:196.
11. McCutchan, *Mier Expedition Diary*, 108.
12. Ibid.
13. Nance, *Dare-Devils All*, 418.
14. Norman Woods to brothers and sisters, etc., October 17, 1843, Spellman, ed., "Letters of the 'Dawson Men,'" *SHQ* 38: 267.

Chapter 42: Bigfoot Is Freed
1. Haynes, *Soldiers of Misfortune*, 186, from Thompson to Upshur, March 25, 1844, *Diplomatic Correspondence of the United States: Inter-American Affairs, 1831-1860*, 8:581.

Chapter 43: The Men Left Behind
1. One of the men was Governor McDowell of Virginia, a neighbor and old friend.
2. Sowell, *Big Foot*, 111. The other three men were Thomas Tatum, William F. Wilson, and James Armstrong.
3. Sowell, *Big Foot*, 112.
4. Bartlett, *Those Valiant Texans*, 149.
5. Ibid.

Chapter 44: Doña Inés de Santa Anna Dies
1. Haynes, *Soldiers of Misfortune*, 196, from McCutchan, *Mier Expedition Diary*, 142-143.
2. Day, *Black Beans*, 31.

Chapter 45: Santa Anna Is Persuaded
1. Fehrenbach, *Fire and Blood*, 390.

Chapter 46: What Happened to John C. C. Hill and Bigfoot Wallace?
1. McCutchan, *Mier Expedition Diary*, 144n.
2. Smithwick, *The Evolution of a State*, 205.
3. Haynes, *Soldiers of Misfortune*, 197.
4. Haynes, *Soldiers of Misfortune*, 199, from McCutchan, *Mier Expedition Diary*, 148.
5. Navarro was a native of San Antonio, a prominent landowner, and one of three Mexicans to sign the Texas Declaration of Independence in 1836.
6. Haynes, *Soldiers of Misfortune*, 202.
7. Smithwick, *The Evolution of a State*, 205.
8. Haynes, *Soldiers of Misfortune*, 202. In all, the edict of September 16, 1844, freed 120 prisoners: 104 from Perote, 2 from Matamoros, 1 from Puebla, 3 from Mexico City, and 10 from Veracruz. Haynes cites Shannon to Calhoun, September 21, 1844, No. 2, National Archives: Despatches from United States Ministers to Mexico, volume 12.

Chapter 47:
1. Nance, *Attack and Counterattack*, 302 from Wharton Jackson Green, *Recollections and Reflections*, 129-130.
2. Sowell, *Early Settlers*, 84.
3. Ibid.
4. Ibid., 85.

Glossary

alcalde	a city official similar to a mayor
aguardiente	liquor or "fire water"
bandidos	Spanish for bandits
buckskin	thin, soft leather
burra	Spanish for a female donkey
cabrito	Spanish for "little goat" used to refer to roasted goat meat
chaparral	shrub brush
cornshucking	taking exterior leaves from ears of corn
Creole	in Mexico this refers to Mexicans of European descent
diezmo	killing one person in ten
grapeshot	small pellets contained in a large shell or cartridge
grub	food
Hijito	Spanish for *sonny*
hombre	Spanish for *man*
hombrecito	Spanish for *little man*
leggings	a thick covering usually from the ankle to the knee, but sometimes higher, usually made of leather or canvas, wrapped or buckled around the legs for protection

Lipan Apache	one of several different bands belonging to the large Apache Indian tribe native to the American southwest. Along with the Mescalero Apache, the Lipan Apache lived primarily in the western part of Texas and eastern New Mexico.
machete	a thick, sword like blade for hacking
maguey	a thick-leaved cactus
muster	gather together
Muster Oak	a specific oak tree in La Grange, Texas where the volunteers gathered
peltries	animal hides; this is Wallace's personal version of
probrecito	Spanish for *poor little thing*; the *ito* may denote affection of helplessness as it does in this case
presidio	fort
prickly pear	the fruit of a cactus
quarter	mercy "no quarter" means no mercy will be granted; the captive will be killed
Quién viva	Spanish for "who lives" used instead of "who goes there"
swashbuckling	show-off as dashing, manly, and tough
Tejana	Female Texas of Hispanic descent
Tejanos	Texans of Hispanic descent
tenpin	bowling pin

Bibliography

Bartlett, Robert M. *Those Valiant Texans – A Breed Apart*. Portsmouth, N.H.: Peter E. Randall Publisher, 1989.
Bell, Thomas W. *A Narrative of the Capture and Subsequent Sufferings of the Mier Prisoners*. N.Y.: 1845. Waco: Texian Press, 1964.
Caldecott, Wilfred H. *Santa Anna, The Story of the Enigma Who Once Was Mexico*. Norman: University of Oklahoma Press, 1936.
Carroll, J. M. *History of Texas Baptists*. Dallas: Baptist Standard Publishing, 1923.
Conner, Seymour V. "Perote Prison," *Handbook of Texas Online*. http://www.tsha.utexas.edu/handbook/online/articles/view/PP/jjp2.html (December 27, 2007).
Cutrer, Thomas W. *Ben McCulloch and the Frontier Military Tradition*. Chapel Hill: University of North Carolina Press, 1993.
Cutrer, Thomas W. "Cameron, Ewen" *Handbook of Texas Online*. http://www.tsha.utexas.edu/handbook/online/articles/CC/fca25.html (December 27, 2007).
Day, James M. *Black Beans and Goose Quills, Literature of the Texan Mier Expedition*. Waco: Texian Press, 1970.
Day, James M. "Black Beans and Dry Bones" (Speech given to the El Paso Corral of the Westerners Club on December 12, 1970.) http://digitalcommons.utep.edu/cgi/viewcontent.cgi?article=1049&context=interviews. Accessed on December 27, 2009.
Duval, John C. *The Adventures of Big Foot Wallace*. Edited by Mabel Major and Rebecca Smith Lee, *Bison Book*. Lincoln: University of Nebraska Press, 1966 replica of the 1936 edition.
———. *Big-Foot Wallace, The Texas Ranger and Hunter*. Southern District of Georgia: J. W. Burke & Co, 1870.
Eisenhower, John S. D. *So Far from God, The U.S. War with Mexico, 1846-1848*. New York: Random House, 1989.
Erath, George B. *Memoirs of George B. Erath, 1818-1891*. Waco: Heritage Society of Waco, 1956.
Erath, George B. "Memoirs of George B. Erath," Edited by Lucy Erath,

Southwestern Historical Quarterly 25 (1922-1923): 207-233, 255-279; 27(1923-1924): 27-51.

Fehrenbach, T. R. *Comanches, The Destruction of a People.* New York: Da Capo Press, 1994.

Fehrenbach, T. R. *Fire and Blood: A History of Mexico.* New York: Macmillan Press, 1973.

Fehrenbach, T. R. *Lone Star: A History of Texas and the Texans.* New York: Macmillan Press, 1980.

Gooch-Iglehart, Fanny Chambers. *The Boy Captive of the Texas Mier Expedition.* J. R. Wood:1909.

Green, Rena Maverick. *Samuel Maverick, Texas: 1803-1870.* San Antonio: Privately printed, 1952.

Green, Thomas J. *Journal of the Texas Expedition Against Mier.* Edited by Sam W. Haynes. Austin: W. Thomas Taylor, 1993.

Greer, James Kimmins. *Colonel Jack Hays Texas Frontier Leader and California Builder.* College Station: Texas A&M University Press, 1987. (Originally New York: Dutton, 1952)

Harper, Jo. *Bigfoot Wallace: Texas Ranger and Mier Survivor.* Austin: Eakin Press, 1997.

Harper, Jo. *Deaf Smith: Scout, Spy, and Texas Hero.* Austin: Eakin Press, 1996.

Haynes, Sam W. *Soldiers of Misfortune, The Somervell and Mier Expeditions.* Austin: University of Texas Press, 1990.

Hardin, Stephen and Richard Hook. *The Texas Rangers.* London: Osprey Publishing, Ltd., 1991.

Hendricks, Sterling B. "The Somervell Expedition to the Rio Grande, 1842," *Southwestern Historical Quarterly* 23 (October 1919)

Herring, Hubert. *A History of Latin America.* New York: Alfred A. Knopf, 1967.

Hunter, John Warren. *Adventures of a Mier Prisioner: Being the Thrilling Experiences of John Rufus Alexander, Who Was with the Ill-Fated Expedition Which Invaded Mexico.* Bandera: Frontier Times, n.d.

Jenkins, John Holland. *Recollections of Early Texas: The Memories of John Holland Jenkins.* Edited by John Holmes Jenkins III. Austin: University of Texas Press, 1958.

Lane, Walter P. *The Adventures and Recollections of a San Jacinto Veteran.* Marshall: Tri-Weekly Herald, 1887.

McCutchan, Joseph D. *Mier Expedition Diary: A Texas Prisoner's Account.* Edited by Joseph Milton Nance. Austin: University of Texas Press, 1978.

Marks, Paula Mitchell. *Turn Your Eyes Toward Texas, Pioneers Sam and Mary Maverick.* College Station: Texas A&M University Press, 1989.

Morrell, Zenos N. *Flowers and Fruits in the Wilderness.* Waco: Baylor University Press, 1976.

Nance, Joseph Milton. *After San Jacinto, The Texas-Mexican Frontier, 1836-1841.* Austin: University of Texas Press, 1963.

Nance, Joseph Milton. *Attack and Counter-Attack, The Texas-Mexican Frontier, 1842.* Austin: University of Texas Press, 1964.

Nance, Joseph Milton. *Dare-Devils All, The Texas Mier Expedition*. Edited by Archie P. McDonald. Austin: Eakin Press, 1998.

Newcomb, W.W., Jr. *The Indians of Texas*. Austin: University of Texas Press, 1961.

O'Brien, Steven. *Antonio Lopez De Santa Anna*. N.Y.: Chelsea House, 1992.

Ramsey, James. "Manuscript of the Mexican War." *Republic of Texas Index* http://www.tamu.edu/ccbn/dewitt/salado.htm. (16 Oct. 1998).

Rittenhouse, J. D. *Maverick Tales, True Stories of Early Texas*. New York: Winchester Press, 1971.

Sinks, Julia Lee. *Chronicles of Fayette*. LaGrange, Texas: *LaGrange Journal*, 1936.

Smithwick, Noah. *The Evolution of a State or Recollections of Old Texas Days*. Austin: University of Texas Press, 1984.

Sowell, Andrew Jackson. *Early Settlers and Indian Fighters of Southwest Texas*. Austin: State House Press, 1986. Also available online at http://books.google.com. Accessed January 29, 2010.

Sowell, Andrew Jackson. *Life of "Big Foot" Wallace*. Austin: State House Press, 1989, replica of the 1899 edition.

Spellman, L. U., ed. "Letters of the 'Dawson Men' from Perote Prison, Mexico, 1842-1843." *Southwestern Historical Quarterly* 38 (April 1935): 246-269.

Spellman, Paul N. "Zadock and Minerva Cottle Woods, American Pioneers." Master's thesis, University of Texas at Austin, 1987, 129.

Stapp, William Preston. *The Prisoners of Perote*. Austin: University of Texas Press, 1997.

Thompson, Waddy. *Recollections of Mexico*. N.Y.: Wiley and Putnam, 1846.

Trueheart, James I. *The Perote Prisoners: Being the Diary of James L. Truehart*. Edited by Frederick C. Chabot. San Antonio: Naylor Col., 1932.

Wade, Houston. *Notes and Fragments of the Mier Expedition*. La Grange, Texas: *La Grange Journal*, 1936.

Walker, Samuel. *Samuel Walker's Account of the Mier Expedition*. Edited by Marilyn McAdams Sibley. Austin: State Historical Association, 1978.

Webb, Walter Prescott. *The Texas Rangers, A Century of Frontier Defense*. Austin, University of Texas Press, 1965.

Weyand, Leonie R., and Houston Wade. *An Early History of Fayette County*. La Grange, Texas: *La Grange Journal*, 1936

Wilsom, William F. "Two Letters from a Mier Prisoner." *Texas State Historical Association Quarterly* 2 (January 1899) 233-236.

Winkler, E. W., ed, "The Bexar and Dawson Prisoners." *Texas State Historical Association Quarterly* 13 (1909-1910) 292-324.

Wright, Muriel H. *A Guide to the Indian Tribes of Oklahoma*. Norman, Oklahoma: University of Oklahoma Press, 1951.

Zumwalt, Captain Adam. "Battle of Salado." Republic of Texas-Index. http://www.tamu.edu/ccbn/dewitt/salado.htm (16 Oct 1998).

Index

Ackland, Kit, 30
Adams, John, 200
Alamo, Battle of the, 12
Alexander, John Rufus, 105, 108, 120, 121, 122, 131, 199, 200
Alexander, Mary Fisher Jones, 200
Allen, Isaac, 153, 177, 178
Ampudia, Captain (brother to Gen), 196, 197
Ampudia, Don Miguel, 80, 82
Ampudia, Pedro de, 56, 61, 62, 63, 65, 68, 70, 71, 72, 73, 74, 75, 76, 77, 79, 80, 81, 82, 85, 86, 87, 92, 93, 95, 97, 98, 99, 100, 141, 142, 145, 154, 156, 160, 192, 193, 196
annexation of Mexican territory, 36
Arredondo, Lieutenant, 110
Atascosa, 44
Austin, Stephen F., 52
Austin, Texas, 6

Barber, James, 85
Barragán, Lieutenant, 108, 109
Barragán, Manuel, 104, 107, 108, 110, 111, 113
Bartlett, Robert M., vii
Battleground Prairie, 203
Beale, Robert Harper, 89
Beard, Robert, 129, 131
Beard, William, 129, 131
Berry, Bate, 69, 104, 108
Berry, Joseph, 66, 69
Bidler, John, 89
Billingsley, Jesse, 24, 28

Biscinia, General, 125, 126
black bean drawing, 129
Boca de los Tres Rios, 123
Bocanegra, Jose Maria, 147
Bogart, Captain, 39
Bowman, Sellers & Company, 204
Bradley, John, 34
Bravo, Nicolas, 127
Brenham, Richard F., 105, 108
Brennan, John, 92
Bruce, Robert, 197
Brush, Gilbert, 43, 99, 154, 157, 161, 182, 189, 199, 200
Buckner's Creek, 3, 4, 14
Burleson, Edward, 89
Buster, Claudius, 67, 118, 125, 126

Calderon, Fanny, 144
Caldwell, Mathew "Old Paint," 11, 12, 13, 15, 17, 18, 19, 21-22, 23, 25, 28, 30, 32, 33
Calleja, General, 128
Camargo, Mexico, 93
Cameron, Ewen, 20, 42, 43, 55, 62, 72, 73, 78, 97, 106, 107, 108, 109, 113, 114, 115, 116, 118, 123, 124, 129, 130, 134, 139, 154, 156, 158, 189
Cameron, John, 113, 114
Canales Rosillo, Antonio, 56, 61, 62, 97, 104
Canfield, Israel, 75, 129
captives' deprivation and abuses, 31, 45-46, 49, 51, 57, 92, 93, 96, 104, 116, 125, 148, 180

Carrasco, Colonel, 26, 27, 33
Carrizo Indians, 21, 53, 94
Carroll, Parson, 19
Cash, John L., 120, 131
Castle of San Carlos, 157
Castro, Capt., 81
Chalk, Whitfield, 73, 77, 199, 200-201
Chapultepec Military Academy, 82, 144
Chase, Franklin E., 164
Cherokee Indians, 20, 21
Clark, Lieutenant, 157
Cocke, James D., 131
Cockrell, Simon, 20
cold flour, 13
Colorado River, 3, 11
Colquhoun, Ludovic, 175
Colt, Samuel, 205
Comanche Indians, 197, 205
Cook, Colonel, 52
Copeland, Willis, 169, 170
Cordova, Vicente, 20, 21
Costilla, Miguel Hidalgo y, 1
Crawford, Robert Michael, 172
Creole, 187
Creoles, 128, 193
Crockett, Davy, 12, 73
Cuidad Mier, Battle of, 1, 68-79, 93, 106, 118, 141, 142, 143, 147, 150, 154, 165

Dallas Morning News, 202
Dalrymple, John, 178
Davis, Campbell, 182, 183
Davis, Henry, 49
Davis, Tom, 124
Dawson Massacre, 24-27, 28, 29, 33, 34, 39, 101, 185
Dawson, Nicholas Mosby, 11, 15, 24
decimation, 128
Diaz, Jose Porfirio, 196
Dillon, John Thomas, 117
Dixie Grays, 200
Dolores, Mexico, 1
Duval, John C., 7, 41

Eastland, William M., 55, 114, 130
Elliot, Charles, 50
Elliot, Mrs., 28
Erath, George B., 53, 57, 64, 77
Este, Edward, 133

Fannin, James W., 41
Fayetteville, Texas, 7
fire eaters, 43, 55, 57, 60, 65, 70, 76, 81, 82, 87, 92, 94, 98, 99, 106, 112, 141, 142, 154, 155, 156, 157, 158, 161, 189, 193
Fisher, William S., 55, 56, 57, 59, 60, 62, 72, 74, 75, 76, 77, 82, 83, 87, 92, 97, 98, 100, 101, 103, 104, 105, 107, 110, 149, 150, 151, 157, 174, 199, 201
Fitzgerald, John, 172
Flacco, 14-15, 47, 48, 55, 56, 57, 88, 89, 90
Fort Oldham, 203
Fruits and Flowers from the Wilderness, 203

Galveston Cotton Exchange, 204
Galveston New Wharf and Cotton Press Company, 204
Garcia Mansion, 80
Garland, Hamlin, 197
Gattis, D. H., 169, 170, 171
Gibson, F. M., 129, 131
Gil, Juan Cristobal Colon, see John C.C. Hill
Glasscock, James, 75, 117
Goliad, Battle of, 41, 77
Gonzales, Texas, 3, 11, 24, 53
Gooch-Inglehart, Fanny Chambers, vii
Green, Thomas Jefferson, 50, 52, 53, 55, 57, 58, 59, 61, 65, 66, 67, 70, 73, 75, 76, 78, 81, 82, 83, 85, 87, 92, 97, 98, 100, 101, 103, 104, 105, 106, 107, 110, 149, 150, 151, 157, 174, 175, 176, 177, 178, 179, 198, 199, 201
Green, Wharton J., 198

Index 233

Griffin, Joe, 15-16, 25, 34
Guadalupe, Mexico, 170
Guerrero (village), 51, 52, 53

Hacienda de Salado, 105, 107, 110, 112, 113, 122, 127, 128, 129, 150, 154, 158, 174, 180, 200, 203
Harlan, Delia, 203
Harrell, Milvern, 11, 101, 103, 112, 185, 200, 202
Hays, Jack Coffee, 5, 13, 14, 17, 18, 29, 30, 31, 47, 53, 55, 61, 199, 201-202, 204, 205
Hays, Lewis, 89
Hendricks, S. B., 47
Henrie, Daniel Drake, 98, 157, 178
Hidalgo Hotel, 199
Higgerson, John, 101, 103
Highsmith, Ben, 31, 32
Hill, Abraham "Asa," 8, 15, 39, 55, 57, 66, 78, 80, 85, 86, 92, 98, 100, 123, 133, 137, 141, 154, 158, 159, 161, 162, 167, 200, 202
Hill, Alberto, 197
Hill, Angelito, 197
Hill, Augustina Sagredo, 196, 197
Hill, Carlos, 197
Hill, James Monroe, 8, 9, 79, 81
Hill, Jeffrey Barksdale, 8, 15, 39, 45, 55, 57, 66, 70, 78, 81, 82, 85, 86, 92, 141, 159, 164, 165, 167, 168, 200, 202
Hill, John C.C., vii, 1, 8, 9, 15, 39, 42, 43, 45, 55, 57, 60, 65, 66, 70, 78, 80, 81, 82, 85, 86, 92, 94, 95, 99, 100, 133, 141-146, 154, 155, 156, 157, 158, 159, 160, 162, 178, 190, 192, 193, 195-197
Hill, Maclovia, 197
Hill, Mary Ann Murray Masterson, 197
Hill family, 7, 8, 24
Hondo River fight, 29, 30, 32, 33, 34, 39, 73
Hospital de Jesus Nazarene, 155, 158

Houston, Sam, 5, 11, 12, 14, 36, 37, 38, 50, 52, 56, 89, 90, 178, 184
Huehuetoca, 139
Huerta, Domingo, 129, 133
Hutchinson, Judge, 149

J. H. Brower & Co., 204
Jackson, Andrew, 11
Jalapa, Mexico, 184, 186
Jarero, General, 194
Jim Dandy (pony), 45
Johnson, — — (ranger), 6, 7
Jones, J. L., 131, 149, 150
Jones, John, 67
Jones, Mary Fisher, 200
Jouett, Steve, 20
Journeay, —-, 151
Juarez, Benito, 196

Keene, E. Y., 168
Kerlick, John, 205
Kinney, Henry Lawrence, 89

La Grange, Texas, 11, 15, 24, 26, 77
Lamar, Mirabeau B., 3
Laredo, 44, 47, 48-50, 51, 52, 58, 59, 118, 119, 121, 185
Lipan Apaches, 5, 14, 47, 90
Longstreet, Gen., 204
Lord, George, 52
Luckey, Sam, 30, 31
Lyons, Samuel, 65, 66, 98, 156

MacCredae, John, 101, 102
Magna de Clavo, 144
Mallon, Nathaniel R., 6, 7, 89
Manton, Edward, 179
Manton, Joe, 66-67
Masterson, Mary Ann Murray, 197
Matamoros, 92, 95, 96, 98, 99, 100, 142, 164, 169
Maverick, Elizabeth, 4
Maverick, Mary, 16
Maverick, Samuel A., 1, 3, 4, 8, 15, 16, 31, 34, 35, 37, 38, 53, 59, 147, 148, 149, 155, 184, 185, 200, 202

Maxmillian, 196, 197
Mayfield, Gen., 32
Mayfield, James S., 24, 28, 29
McCaleb, Walter F., 61
McClure's Magazine, 197
McCoy, Green, 22
McCulloch, Ben, 32, 47, 56, 61, 77
McCulloch, Henry, 13, 77
McCutchan, Joseph D., 50, 58, 72, 153, 164, 168, 181, 183
McDade, Samuel, 95
McMahan, Thompson, 89
Medina River, 57, 198
Mejia, Francisco, 34, 116, 127, 128
Mendes, Joseph, 8, 100, 159
Merchants' Insurance Company, 204
Mexican War of Independence, 1, 2
Mexico City, 97, 110, 126, 127, 136, 142, 143, 149, 158, 161, 164, 165, 170, 178, 191
Mier, Battle of, see Cuidad Mier, Battle of
Mier, Mexico, 55, 59, 60, 61, 65, 67
Mier Expedition, 2, 57, 66, 123, 201, 202
Mier captives, 87, 88, 92, 103, 124, 155, 158, 172, 174, 184, 185, 188, 190, 191, 192, 193, 194, 200
Miller, Alsey S., 25, 26, 29
Mineria*, 145, 159, 160, 195
Molina del Rey, 161, 165, 168, 169, 170, 172, 179, 180
Monterrey, Mexico, 98, 100, 101, 104, 199, 201, 204, 205
Moore, William "Talkin' Bill," 133, 138
Morgan, John Day, 42, 47, 48, 85, 87, 97, 98, 99, 164, 171, 172, 200, 202-203
Morgan, Rebecca Rogers, 203
Morrell, Allen H., 3, 11, 12, 15, 26, 27, 28, 29, 32, 185, 203
Morrell, Clearancy, 203
Morrell, Delia Harlan, 203

Morrell, Zenos N., 3, 11, 12, 13, 19, 27, 28, 29, 32, 185, 200, 203
Morrow, William P., 129
Murray, Mary Ann, 195, 197
Murray, Thomas W., 98

Nash's Creek, 26
Navarro, Antonio, 90
Navarro, Jose Antonio, 192
New Orleans, 205
Noble (slave), 96
Nueces River, 45, 46, 56, 57
Nueva Reynosa, 94, 95
Nuevo León, 34, 110, 116

Oakland, California, 201
Odgen, —-, 176
Oldham, W. S., Jr., 203
Oldham, William, 77, 96, 119, 120, 121, 122, 200, 203
Ortega, Jose Maria, 110, 111, 116

Padrajo, Francisco, 164, 165
Paso de Benado, 124
Patterson, W. D., 101, 102
Pedernales River, 205
Perez, Francisco, 59, 60, 64, 65, 66, 67
Perote Castle, vii, 12, 59, 147, 149, 150, 151, 156, 157, 165, 167, 172, 173, 174, 175, 177, 179, 180, 185, 191, 193, 196, 197, 201, 202, 203, 205
Perry, Rufus, 29
Phelps, James A. E., 43, 155
Phelps, Orlando, 43, 55, 92, 98, 99, 112, 154, 155, 200, 204
Phyllis (slave of William Oldham), 203
Pierson, G. W., 114
Pilant, George B., 89
Posada, Archbishop, 143, 190
Presidential Palace, 143, 145, 154, 158, 159
Presidio, 44, 103
Presidio del Rio Grande, 101

Puebla, Mexico, 191
Real del Monte, 171
"Red Caps," 104, 135
Reese, Billy, 43, 92, 98, 99, 106, 112, 154, 155, 156, 157, 174, 200, 204
Reese, Charles Keller, 43, 66, 106, 112, 156, 157, 174, 175, 178, 204
Rice, James O., 6, 7, 88, 89
Rio Alamo, 65, 66
Rio Grande, 45, 47, 51, 53, 56, 57, 60, 64, 77, 90, 92, 106, 113, 118, 121, 169
Rivas, —-, 57
Rogers, Rebecca, 203
Romano, Captain, 107, 110, 111
Rupley, William, 89
Ryan, William, 72, 129

Sagredo, Augustina, 196
Sagredo, Raymon, 196
Salado Creek, Battle of, 13, 15, 17, 18, 19, 20-22, 24, 25, 26, 27, 28, 29, 33, 39, 44, 51
Saltillo, 101, 103, 104, 125, 127, 128, 135, 136
Saluria, Texas, 204
San Antonio, 3, 4, 5, 6, 7, 11, 13, 15, 17, 18, 26, 28, 34, 38, 39, 40, 44, 56, 122, 129, 147, 150, 177
San Fernando, 103
San Fernando de Agua Verde, 35
San Fernando de Rosas, 34
San Jacinto, Battle of, 2, 8, 9, 11, 13, 15, 24, 52, 56, 57, 81, 133, 155
San Juan River, 93
San Luis Potosí, 104, 105, 137, 138
Sanchez, Juan Jose, 136
Santa Anna, Antonio López de, 1, 73, 76, 77, 79, 96, 99, 126, 127, 128, 135, 136, 142, 143, 144, 145, 151, 154, 155, 156, 157, 158, 159, 160, 161, 162, 165, 173, 176, 177, 178, 184, 185, 186, 188, 190, 191, 192, 195, 196
Santa Anna, Inés García de, 145, 157, 159, 162, 190, 191, 195

Santa Fe Expedition, 3, 19, 105
Santiago Tlaltelolco, 158
Scott, Winfield, 201
Seguin, Texas, 12-13, 15
Sellers, Harvey, 43, 92, 99, 154, 157, 161, 200, 204
Sentmanat, Francisco, 192, 193
Shannon, Wilson, 191, 192
Shepherd, James L., 98, 136
Sierra de la Paila, 115
Sierra de las Cruces, 161
Simmons, Sol, 19, 20
Sinnickson, John J., 66, 69, 73, 85-86, 92
Smith, Deaf, 13, 40
Smith, French, 19
Smith, John W., 12
Smith, Robert, 129
Smithwick, Noah, 88
Somervell, Alexander, 37, 38, 40, 44, 48, 49, 50, 51, 52, 53, 54, 55, 56, 57, 88, 200, 204
Sowell, A. J., 7
Sowell, Andrew, 22
St. Clair, Caleb, 64, 65, 77
St. Louis Globe Democrat, 203
Stone, Samuel, 177

Tacubaya, 162
Tacubaya, Mexico, 161
Tampico, 164, 171
Taney, John, 68, 123, 133, 175, 178, 180, 185, 191, 194
Taylor, Marina Rodrigues, 35
Taylor, Zachary, 201, 202, 205
Texas Congress, 36
Texas Rangers, 5, 13, 197, 201, 204, 205
Thompson, Thomas A., 119
Thompson, Waddy, 148, 155, 156, 169, 184, 185, 191
Thompson, William, 125, 171, 172
Those Valiant Texans, vii
Thurmond, Alfred, 129, 135, 139, 140, 188
Tonkawa Indians, 16, 29

Toops, John, 118, 125, 126
Tornel, Augustine, 160
Tornel, Jose Marie, 144, 145, 160
Tornel, Manuel, 160
Torrey, — —, 131, 133
Trahern, George Washington, 108, 117, 138
Trimble, Tecolote, 176, 183
Trimble, William, 35, 157
Trinidad, Don, 94
Trueheart, James L., 179, 181
Twohig, John, 4, 176, 178

University of California, 201
Urrea, General, 41

Valle, Guillermo, 99
Van Horn, William H., 117
Vasquez, General, 2
Veracruz, 127, 165, 169, 172, 178, 186, 187, 201
Victoria, Don Guadalupe, 157
Villareal, Florencio, 48, 49

Walker Colt, 205
Walker, Sam, 29, 64, 65, 169, 170, 171, 200, 205
Walker's Creek, 205
Wallace, Bigfoot
Wallace, William Alexander "Bigfoot," 1, 6, 7, 12, 14, 17, 21, 30, 31, 41, 42, 45, 47, 48, 49, 55, 56, 57, 61, 64, 68, 69, 72, 75, 77, 78, 84, 85, 92-93, 108, 109, 113, 115, 116, 119, 124, 125, 129, 133, 134, 136, 137, 162, 179, 180, 181, 182, 186, 187, 197-199
Washington-on-the-Brazos, 40
Webber's Prairie, 88
Weeks, Henry D., 72, 89
Whaling, Henry, 21, 43, 129, 131, 135
Wilson, James C., 169, 170, 171
Wilson, John, 26
Wilson, William F., 129
Woll, Adrián, 2, 4, 7, 11, 15, 17, 27, 28, 29, 30, 32, 101, 150, 176, 185
Woods, Henry Gonzalvo, 11, 26, 27, 167, 168, 205
Woods, Jane, 167, 205
Woods, Norman, 11, 25, 26, 27, 101, 102, 103, 112, 167, 183, 185, 202, 205
Woods, Zadock, 11, 25, 26, 28
Woods' Fort, 11
Wren, Nick, 30

Yocum, Jessie, 43, 60
Young, John, 177
Yucatán, 192

About the Authors

JO HARPER is an acclaimed storyteller who has been referred to as "a female Mark Twain." Her family was one of the first three families to settle in the Texas Panhandle, and she carries on the Texas frontier tradition thruogh her tall tales and her stories about Texas history. She lives in Houston with her family and teaches English at Houston Community College.

JOSEPHINE HARPER, like the mother she was named for, loves both the written and oral literary traditions. Writing history and fiction is her favorite recreation and provides a respite from her work as a clinical psychologist.